EASIER GOLF

PETER ALLISS AND PAUL TREVILLION

STANLEY PAUL | LONDON

STANLEY PAUL & CO LTD
3 Fitzroy Square, London W1

AN IMPRINT OF THE HUTCHINSON GROUP

London Melbourne Sydney Auckland
Wellington Johannesburg Cape Town
and agencies throughout the world

First published August 1969
Second impression February 1971
Third impression July 1973

Printed in Great Britain by litho on antique wove paper
by Anchor Press, and bound by Wm. Brendon,
both of Tiptree, Essex

ISBN 0 09 095940 X

CONTENTS

INTRODUCTION 7

1 THE GRIP 9

2 THE STANCE 16

3 THE FUNDAMENTALS OF THE GOLF
SWING 27

4 THE TEE-SHOT 38

5 FAIRWAY WOODS 43

6 THE LONG IRONS 49

7 THE MEDIUM IRONS 52

8 THE SHORT IRONS 56

9 THE WEDGE 61

10 PUTTING 64

11 BUNKER SHOTS 73

12 PLAYING THE COURSE   81

13 UPHILL, DOWNHILL AND SIDEHILL
        LIES   84

14 PLAYING IN WINDY CONDITIONS   89

15 WET-WEATHER GOLF   95

16 GETTING OUT OF TROUBLE   99

17 SPECIAL SHOTS FOR SPECIAL
        OCCASIONS   104

18 COMMON FAULTS   109

19 THE RIGHT SWING FOR YOUR BUILD   116

20 THE CORRECT WAY TO PRACTISE   120

21 THE MENTAL APPROACH   124

22 CARE OF EQUIPMENT   133

23 WINTER EXERCISES   137

24 THE RULES   140

INTRODUCTION

From the age of fourteen months, when I started hitting a ping-pong ball up and down the garden with a two-foot-long wooden club, golf has been my life. As a boy I spent every spare minute playing golf, no other sport interested me. I never played cricket, football, rugby or tennis—I never learned to swim, skate or ride a horse. Possibly I've missed a lot and yet I don't feel cheated. Not only has golf given me countless hours of enjoyment, it has also provided me with a very fair living.

By the age of fifteen I was a scratch golfer. My game was based on rhythm and timing plus, of course, some sound advice given me by my father. He insisted that golf was a simple game which only the golfers made difficult.

How true this is. Unfortunately too many weekend golfers are not satisfied with a simple, but very effective swing—they demand more. Driven on by this desire, they study every kind of golf theory available, each little gimmick and trick being carefully noted.

But all they succeed in doing is to make a simple game complicated. Gradually even the most straightforward shot becomes a major production. They begin to create for themselves problems which do not exist and their game suffers. Many golfers who have wandered off onto this fruitless path have come to me desperately seeking a solution for their self-created problems.

From the moment I strip their swings of all the unnecessary frills, golf becomes easy for them again. Having solved their problems I began thinking about solving those of others and I decided one of the best ways of doing this would be through an instructional golf book.

What form the book would take posed no problems. It had to have clear, easy-to-understand drawings and diagrams linked together with short, simple explanations. This had to be a book which a person, handling a club for the first time, could pick up, read, understand and put into practice. It had to help the beginner and, just as important, add that vital something extra to the scratch player's game.

From the beginning I had only one artist in mind—Paul Trevillion. Way back in 1962, we had worked together on a newspaper series featuring the Open. I knew he enjoyed golf, played golf and had proved himself just about the best illustrator in this field. We discussed the idea over a round of golf and agreed that such a book was possible, but only if we worked together closely as a team. From that day on we spent many weeks out on the golf course, back in the studio and over the typewriter. The weeks became months as each lesson was discussed at great length —illustrations were checked and checked again—we were after perfection in a form easily understandable to all. Finally, after twelve months, in which we demanded the absolute best from each other, both our professional attitudes were satisfied—the book was finished.

In this book we have explained the simple method I employ when playing golf—no tricks, no gimmicks. It's a method which every golfer can explore without his mind being filled with complicated techniques. Golf is a simple, straightforward game, there is no reason to make it difficult—and if you stick to the principles in this book, it never will be.

1

THE GRIP

In my early years I had a most appalling grip. I used to interlock the little finger of my right hand with my left forefinger and my left thumb was actually *behind* my right hand. But that's not all, my right thumb wasn't even on the shaft, instead it rested on the second finger of my right hand. This was a very powerful, but terribly destructive grip, and although I could hit the ball a very long way I couldn't always be sure I'd find it. Every shot I played was a hook and I reached the stage where my score had stopped coming down. I had to do something and my father saw to it that I did. He insisted I changed to the Vardon grip, the one that 99 out of every 100 golfers use today. For six months I cried myself to sleep as I fought and struggled to make the new grip work. At first I couldn't even hit the ball and only succeeded in taking enormous divots; I wasn't swinging the club, I was digging with it. On the occasions I was lucky enough to hit the ball, it flew in a number of weird directions, but never straight. Anger almost forced me to admit defeat, but I stuck at it. Eventually the nightmare was to end and I was rewarded with control, power and accuracy. I had learned the value of a correct grip, it was a lesson I never forgot.

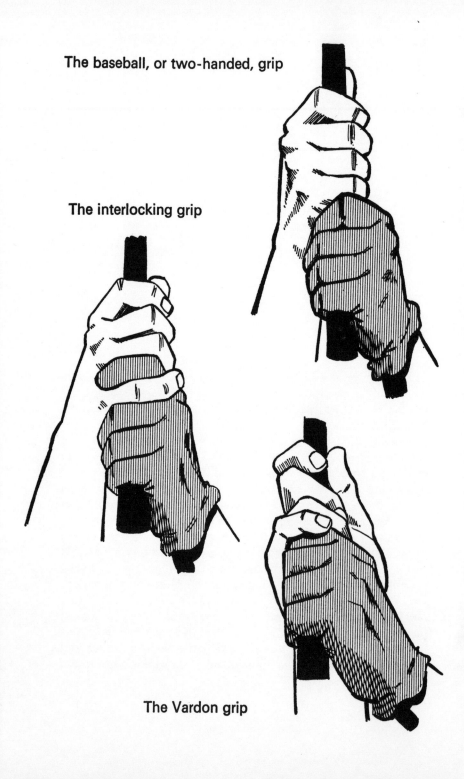

The baseball, or two-handed, grip

The interlocking grip

The Vardon grip

DIFFERENT TYPES OF GRIP

A grip which can control the club throughout the entire swing is essential if you are ever to play golf well. For remember a perfectly controlled swing can never rectify a sloppy hand action caused by an incorrect grip. But a correct grip will allow your hands to rectify a minor fault, during the body movement of the swing.

Golf has introduced many weird and wonderful grips but, generally speaking, only three have stood the test of time. There is the *two-handed grip* favoured by some, including the great Dai Rees. Again, a minority group favour the *interlocking grip* in which the right little finger and left forefinger interlock. Jack Nicklaus is one who employs this grip with staggering success.

But by far the most popular of all is the *Vardon grip*, where the little finger of the right hand hooks over the forefinger of the left. As I have explained, I myself, use the Vardon grip but this is not to say the other two methods are inferior—on the contrary, it has been proved conclusively that one is as good as the other. It's purely a matter of personal choice.

Which of these three grips you decide to use could well depend on the size of your hands. Theoretically it is more comfortable for people with small or weak hands to use either the two-handed or interlocking grip.

THE FINGERS

I am a great believer in getting the club shaft well into the fingers. When one considers the fingers are the most sensitive part of the hands, it is quite logical you should grip the club with them.

Imagine at this moment you are judging the quality of a piece of material, I'm sure, like me, you would hold it between your fingers and thumb. This, of course, is the only way, by feel alone, you can judge it's true value.

So it is with the club shaft, grip it in the fingers and you feel your hands come alive, but if you grip it in the palms your sense of feel is lost and the control over your swing greatly reduced.

THE LEFT HAND

To get the correct grip, stand with your feet shoulder width apart and place the head of the club on the ground behind an imaginary ball. Having done this, place the shaft of the club in your left hand so that it lies diagonally across, starting from the centre of the forefinger to the base of the other three. Now close your fingers as if shaking hands with the club. On looking down at your hand you should see two knuckles. One belonging to the forefinger and

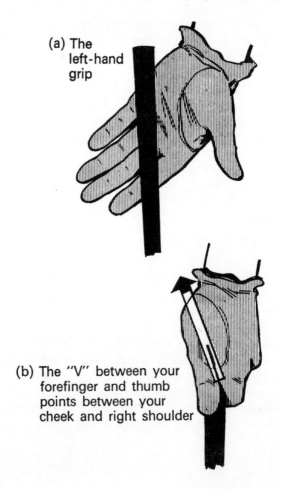

(a) The left-hand grip

(b) The "V" between your forefinger and thumb points between your cheek and right shoulder

the other to the middle finger. Also the 'V' between the forefinger and thumb should be pointing between your cheek and right shoulder. If this is so then all is well.

THE RIGHT HAND

Now place your right hand on the club, taking care that the grip

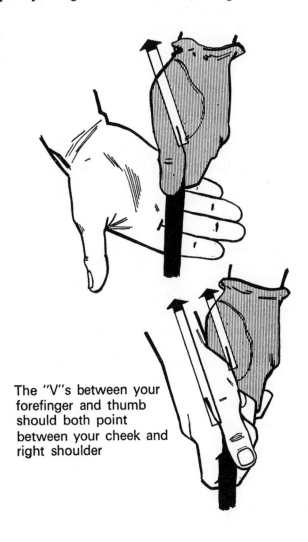

The "V"'s between your forefinger and thumb should both point between your cheek and right shoulder

lies along the base of the fingers. The little finger of the right hand should wrap round the forefinger of the left hand and so unify the two hands into one. In this position the thumb and forefinger of the right hand will form a 'V' pointing between your cheek and right shoulder, just as the thumb and forefinger of the left hand do. Looking down you should see the first and second knuckles of the right hand.

You now have a good sound grip of the club with the hands working together. Many golfers make the mistake of favouring one hand in the swing. This is wrong and can only result in a variety of indifferent shots. *Golf is a two-handed game, never forget this.*

POSSIBLE FAULTS

The club should be held firmly but gently, without setting up any undue tension in the forearm muscles. A very common fault, and one to be avoided is loosening the hands at the top of the backswing (the Piccolo grip); when you tighten up your grip again the position of the clubface is changed, and both length and direction are affected.

Then again, if you have an extra long left thumb which pokes out, your grip is again in danger of being disturbed. Gary Player is one of the many tournament golfers who draw their thumb up the grip to avoid this. *Pull the thumb up, like a tortoise pulls in it's head.* I caught my left thumb in a car door when I was a child and now it's a little bit smaller than my right one. This, of course, is perfect for the golf grip, for when I place my right hand around the shaft, my small left thumb fits snugly into the hollow formed by the palm and thumb of my right hand. So remember, keep your thumb up if you want to keep your score down.

TAKE A TIP . . .

A good way to tell if your grip was correct at impact is to check it at the finish of your swing. For consistent length and direction, your grip must remain unchanged throughout the stroke.

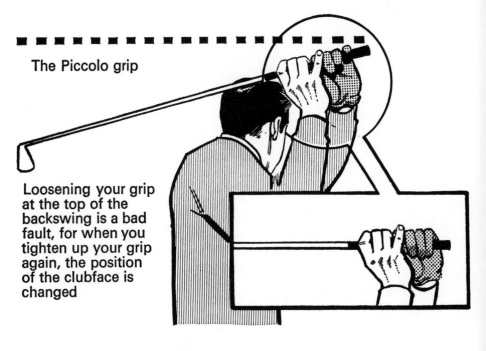

The Piccolo grip

Loosening your grip at the top of the backswing is a bad fault, for when you tighten up your grip again, the position of the clubface is changed

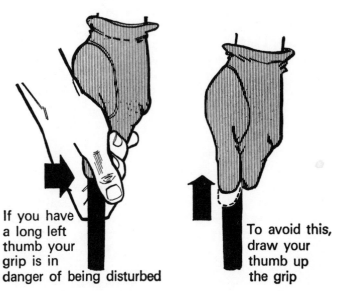

If you have a long left thumb your grip is in danger of being disturbed

To avoid this, draw your thumb up the grip

2

THE STANCE

I am quite sure that only one in every fifty weekend golfers has a correct stance. Most of them have been misled by the so-called magic of 'open' and 'closed' stances. Moving the ball back for the shorter club and keeping the toes pointing to 'five to one' on an imaginary clock dial. One cannot generalise on these things and it would be foolish to attempt to do so. These false doctrines have ruined more golf swings than any other factor in golf. So forget it all, read on and I will show you the stance best suited to your particular physique.

POSITION OF THE FEET

The feet, more than any other part of the body, make the golf swing. The great Sam Snead, rated the finest and most natural swinger ever to step onto a tee, endorses this fact. If your feet are not positioned right when you take your stance, then you're wasting your time taking a club from the bag. All of the common golf problems such as slicing, hooking, pushing, pulling, can, in many cases, be attributed to the feet.

I am a firm believer that you should stand to the ball the way

If, like Charlie Chaplin, you stand with your feet
in a 'quarter to three' position, this is the stance
for you

you put your feet down when you walk. Try it for yourself—throw a golf ball on the ground and then walk up to it. The moment you are standing over the ball look down at your feet. If they point to 'ten to two' on an imaginary clock dial then that's the position of the feet for you. But if you're a 'five to one' walker, like me, then stand that way. I am quite serious when I say that if Charlie Chaplin came to me I would never dream of altering his 'quarter to three' stance. Nor for that matter would I make adjustments to a person who is slightly pigeon-toed. If any of you who saw Henry Cotton play had cared to glance down at his feet you would have noticed he stood up to the ball slightly pigeon-toed—and why not? It was the perfectly correct and sensible thing to do, for Cotton does tend to walk that way. It doesn't take a great mind to understand that the reason you walk in the manner you do is because it provides you with the perfect balance for your own particular build.

Tamper with your feet positions and you destroy the very essence of the golf swing—rhythm and balance.

Now I don't want you to accept all that I have just said simply because my name's Peter Alliss and I have won a tournament or two. In the words of Billy Graham 'I want you to get up and get out of your seat' and experiment for yourself.

(A) Turn both feet well in.

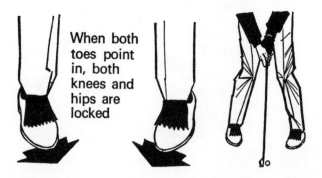

When both toes point in, both knees and hips are locked

Result: You lock both knees and hips. To swing the club becomes almost an impossibility.

(B) Turn both feet out.

When both toes point out, both knees and hips are freed

Result: Now you free both knees and hips and the swing becomes too loose, free and easy.

(C) Point the right foot straight ahead of you and turn the **left** foot out.

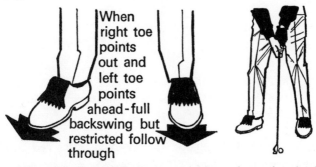

When right toe points out and left toe points ahead-full backswing but restricted follow through

Result: You lock your right knee and hip and restrict the back-swing—but turned left foot frees the left hip and knees and allows a full follow-through.

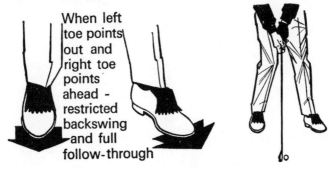

When left toe points out and right toe points ahead - restricted backswing and full follow-through

(D) Point the left foot straight ahead of you and turn the right foot out.

Result: Your turned-out right foot frees the right hip and knee and allows a full easy backswing, but the straight-ahead left foot locks the left hip and knee and restricts the follow-through.

(E) Take a natural stance (the way you walk) and draw the right foot back a couple of inches.

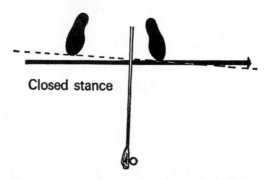

Closed stance

Result: Your free right side permits a nice easy backswing—but your left side will restrict your follow-through. Many golfers adopt this 'closed stance' when setting up for an intentional hook.

(F) Take your natural stance (the way you walk) and this time draw your left foot back a couple of inches.

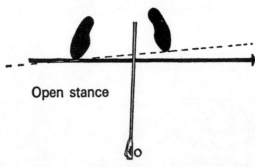

Open stance

Result: Now we have a restricted backswing but the open left side will allow a full easy follow-through. Here again, many golfers adopt this 'open stance' when they want an intentional slice.

From all this it is quite easy to see just how important the feet are. To sum up I strongly recommend all club golfers to adopt a square stance, or one as close to it as possible depending on your physique.

THE SQUARE STANCE

By a square stance I simply mean one where an imaginary line drawn through the heels of the feet and extended towards the hole will be parallel to the line of flight of the ball towards the target. You can easily check it for yourself by placing a club in

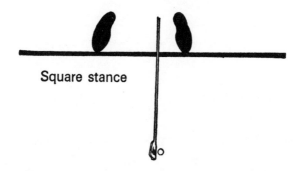

Square stance

front of your toes as you address the shot. Now take a couple of steps back and look to see if the club lies parallel to the target line. If it does your stance is square.

For a full shot with the driver the feet should be a little more than shoulder width apart. For the shorter irons the feet are brought closer together, *but at all times be sure you have a true sense of balance*.

DISTANCE FROM THE BALL

The face of the club must lie squarely behind the ball without you feeling you are reaching for it, or being cramped by standing too close. You should feel nicely balanced with your weight evenly on the balls of both feet. From this position you will be able to swing freely without swaying backwards or falling forward into the shot.

POSITION OF THE BALL

Here again, I believe in keeping it simple. I don't agree with having the ball off your left toe for the woods, in the 'middle' of your stance for the mid-irons and off the right foot for the pitching clubs. There is no point in complicating matters by making constant adjustments in the arc of the swing for the various ball positions. I always keep the ball in the same place for every shot, and that is just inside my left heel. By doing this I create for myself 'The Magic Triangle'.

THE MAGIC TRIANGLE

Imagine a line drawn from your right heel to the ball. A line

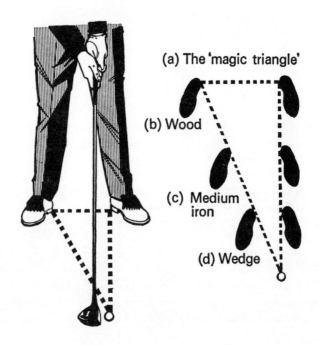

(a) The 'magic triangle'

(b) Wood

(c) Medium iron

(d) Wedge

drawn from your left heel to the ball, then a line drawn joining both heels. This gives you a right-angled triangle. Now all you must remember is to keep your heels on the legs of the triangle when you take a shorter club and move nearer to the ball, with a correspondingly narrow stance.

This, then, is the 'magic triangle'—a conception of my father, Percy Alliss—and one which I recommend, for it is a simple and effective method which never fails.

KNEES

Flex or bend your knees slightly as though you are about to sit down on a high stool.

POSTURE AT ADDRESS

Your body should bend slightly at the waist but not too much as it is wrong to crouch over the ball, for this will not only feel awkward it will stop you hitting the ball with maximum power. The line from the base of the spine to the head should be almost straight.

ARM POSITIONS

The left arm and the shaft of the club should form a straight line extending from the left shoulder to the ball. A word of warning— guard against holding the left arm too rigid. Your right arm should be relaxed and bent at the elbow and close to the body. Keep your hands up, if you drop them there are too many links in the chain and it is possible to hit the ground anywhere within a two-foot radius of the ball.

SHOULDER POSITION

In the correct stance the right shoulder should be slightly lower than the left. This is because the right hand is placed below the left in order to grip the club.

Posture at Address

The line from the base of the spine to head should be almost straight

Keep your hands up

Bend your knees slightly as though you are about to sit on a high stool

HEAD

Hold your head up, never let it sink down in your shoulders like a tortoise and make sure that it does not move. It is essential that you keep your head still throughout the swing and even after the ball is well on it's way.

TAKE A TIP . . .

For some reason many weekend golfers, even if they don't feel right, do not like to change their stance once they have got set to hit the ball. This is a mistake, never be afraid to walk away and come back and re-address the ball.

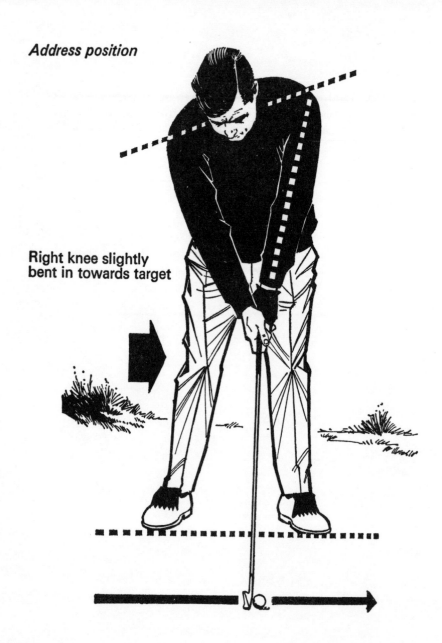

Address position

Right knee slightly
bent in towards target

3

THE FUNDAMENTALS OF THE GOLF SWING

A few years ago a young man with a golf swing problem came to me seeking advice. He was an enormously strong fellow and, as he explained his troubles, he staggered me by the simple way he lifted a desk chair with only one hand. You may not think this very impressive but when you consider I was sitting on it at the time you will appreciate why I was so amazed. His problem was a sad one. Here was a man endowed with tremendous physical strength and yet he couldn't hit a golf ball much more than 150 yards. His muscle power was of no help to him, he lacked the most vital factor in the whole of the golf swing—rhythm.

RHYTHM

It doesn't matter if it's a fast rhythm or a slow rhythm as long as you have it. Jack Nicklaus takes the club back slowly, whereas Arnold Palmer takes it back quickly, yet they both have rhythm. Some golfers are born with a natural rhythm, others have to spend hours on the practice ground trying to acquire it.

To understand why rhythm is so important one has only to think of the sequence of the golf swing: backswing—downswing—

impact—follow through. To co-ordinate all these into one free-flowing movement is not easy, without rhythm it becomes impossible. Now don't start thinking that the golf swing is not a simple action—it is, but never be fooled into thinking that it is an easy one. Remember you're asking the body to perform unnatural movements, so therefore it requires constant practice to find the rhythm which will enable the body to perform these naturally. The person who can do these movements with the greatest rhythm will automatically make it look easy and appear to be a more natural golfer than one who has to constantly struggle with his rhythm in order to get the same result.

That's why such golfers as Sam Snead, the late Tony Lema, Roberto de Vicenzo, Billy Casper and yours truly, have been termed natural golfers. But this, strictly speaking, just isn't so; there is no such thing as a natural golfer. It is the rhythm, not the swing, which is natural and therefore we make the swing appear to be a relatively easy thing. But golfers like Jack Nicklaus, who take a terribly long time to hit the ball, make the swing look difficult. Anybody who takes a long time setting up and requires half a dozen waggles before he hits the ball does look as if he's having trouble with his swing. Jack Nicklaus and Brian Huggett are among those who seem to struggle to find a rhythm. Golfers such as these are quite often spoken of as having artificial or manufactured swings. Whereas a golfer like Billy Casper, who just walks up, no fuss, no frill, and immediately hits off, is automatically tagged a natural golfer.

THE TWIN PLANES OF THE GOLF SWING

In the golf swing the trunk movement is more or less parallel to the ground, whereas the arm action is more or less perpendicular to the ground. These then, are the twin planes of the golf swing, two entirely separate movements. The body rotating one way and the arms swinging another.

I have always likened my own particular swing to that of a windmill. The body of the windmill being my body—the sails of the windmill being my arms. My main object during the swing is to keep the arc as wide as possible. My arms must extend the club away from my body to give the clubhead a free-flowing movement throughout the entire swing. This means I have a consistent swing arc which repeats itself every time.

THE BACKSWING

I agree with Sam Snead that it is a mistake to become too involved in the mechanics of the swing when you first start to play golf. If I had done so, I am convinced I would be only an average golfer today. Many club golfers, when they are practising their golf, waste time by keep stopping to look round to check their backswing. They worry about the position of their hands at the top, whether the clubface is open or shut. In most cases this does more harm than good. They should be thinking only of hitting that ball to the target. That's the most important part—ball-target.

All of us, at one time or another, have thrown a ball of some sort. Now ask yourself, did you worry about how you took your arm back? Did you look round to see if you were holding it correctly? Of course not. You only thought in a forward direction —ball to target. It's the same when playing darts. Do good players look back? No.

If you have checked that everything is right before you start the actual swing there should be no reason for re-checking at the top of the backswing.

THE TAKE-AWAY

Guard against starting the first two feet of the backswing too quickly for this is the quickest way of upsetting the whole rhythm of the swing. Arnold Palmer, Dai Rees, and Charlie Ward all have exceptionally fast swings, but they always start smoothly and *then* accelerate. Obviously the speed tempo of the swing will depend on the individual—for some it will be fast, for others slow—but in both cases the first essential step of the swing will be a smooth, unhurried take-away. Don't pick the club up with the hands, swing it slowly and smoothly straight back from the ball or even slightly inside the line of flight, keeping it low along the ground. By doing it this way you automatically keep your left arm straight and fully extended, which results in a nice wide

Keep the first two feet of the take-away slow and smooth. Knees remain bent—arms only move

swing arc. Don't for one moment think the take-away is simply a hand and arm movement. Of course, it will feel like that, but actually the take-away is a 'one-piece' movement in which the golfer's whole body—hands, arms, shoulders and trunk—move as one.

THE SHOULDER TURN

Make sure you have a really good shoulder turn. Ideally the left shoulder should pass under the chin and your back should be facing the target. Forget about your hips, a correct shoulder turn will see to it that they play their part. You have noticed I have stressed the word *turn*—and that is precisely what I mean. Do not *sway* to the side during the backswing for this will alter the position of the head and ruin your swing.

TOP OF THE BACKSWING

At the top of your backswing about sixty per cent of your weight should now be on your right foot and your right elbow should be pointing to the ground. Now a word of caution—the majority of club golfers tend to overswing. If you find that you have been forced to relax your grip in order to complete the backswing, the

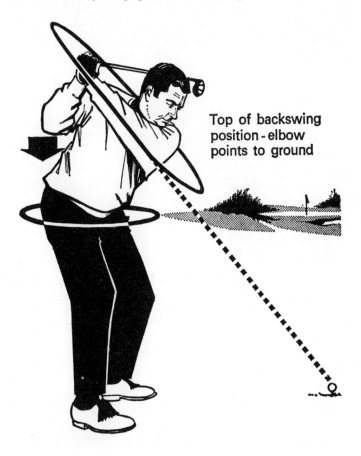

Top of backswing
position - elbow
points to ground

chances are you are overswinging. Personally I feel the club should never drop below the horizontal—in fact you can generate tremendous clubhead speed from a three-quarter backswing.

THE DOWNSWING

It is a mistake to start the downswing with the hands 'hitting from the top'—not only do you release your built up power too soon, but both timing and rhythm are lost.

Start the downswing with your left hip. Then the left shoulder, left arm and last of all the hands. At all times you should feel that your hands are *following* and not *leading* in the downswing.

Because of the muscular tension built up during the backswing, you will automatically come down fast and your weight will move to the left side.

THE FEET

At impact my right heel is off the ground and my right knee has moved towards the target. My left leg has straightened to brace itself against the sudden weight shift. Keep the left foot firmly on the ground to resist the power surge of the weight transference. Now you can see what an important part the feet play. I cannot over-emphasise their importance for I firmly believe that every good swing is built on the foundation of correct footwork.

IMPACT

Make sure that your hands are ahead of the clubhead until the last possible moment before impact. Then the clubhead must catch up to meet the ball. Keep the clubface square to the line of flight and low along the ground for several inches following impact.

THE FOLLOW-THROUGH

As you hit through the ball keep the right arm extended and pointing to the target for as long as possible. Only when the arms have reached waist level should they begin to cross over your body. At the completion of your swing your hands should be high up

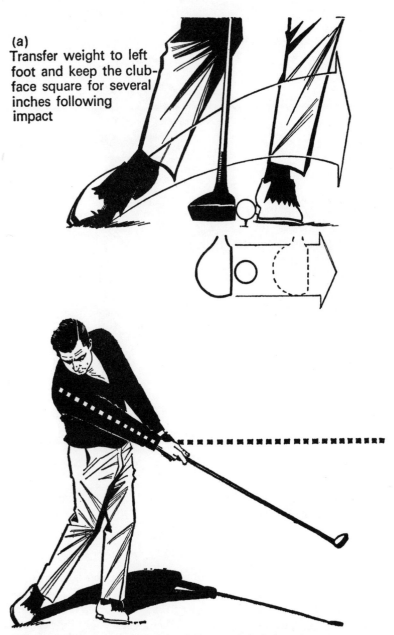

(a)
Transfer weight to left foot and keep the club-face square for several inches following impact

(b) Hit through the ball and keep the right arm extended and pointing to target for as long as possible

Completion of follow
through. Right knee
points to flag
weight transferred to
left foot

with your body facing the target and, most important, you should
be perfectly balanced.

THE HEAD

Keeping the head still throughout the swing demands all of your
concentration, so remember, stare down hard at the ball at address
and keep on staring down at it during the swing. Even after impact
you should still be staring down and then, when your club is about
parallel to the ground, the natural force of the swing will pull

The angle of hips and shoulders throughout the full swing

your head, both up and round, to a position from which you can
follow the ball's flight. It was said that Ben Hogan never hit a ball
until he had *outstared* it!

One of the surest ways of ruining a golf swing is by moving the
head—this is a fact which you can easily prove for yourself.
Take a short piece of string and tie a loop at each end. Place a
drawing pin through one loop and pin it to a postcard. Now put
a pencil through the other loop and prescribe an arc below the
pin. At the lowest point of the arc draw a small circle to represent

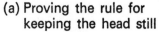

(a) Proving the rule for
keeping the head still

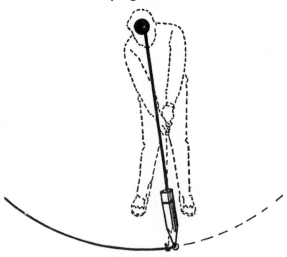

(b) Result of moving
head up or down

(c) Result if head is
moved to either side

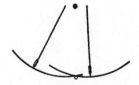

the golf ball. As long as the pin (which represents the golfer's head) remains in that position the swing of the arc will always cut through the centre of the 'ball'. But move the pin in any direction, be it up, down or to the side, and the arc of the swing will miss the ball. So it is with the head. If you do not maintain it's address position through the swing you are in serious trouble. Remember the head is the only part of the anatomy which does not move during the golf swing.

TAKE A TIP . . .

'Right elbow close to the body'—this can, if misinterpreted, lead to all sorts of restrictions—no width in the backswing and a general lack of power. Also the right arm can straighten too soon and result in a hit behind the ball. As long as your right elbow points to the ground, there is no reason why it should not leave your side during the backswing.

4

THE TEE-SHOT

The average weekender wants to come out, stride onto the first tee, take out his driver and bang the ball 250 yards right down the middle. Well, this just isn't on. I wouldn't back myself to do that if I hadn't handled a club for a week. And let's be fair, possibly the heaviest thing the average club golfer picks up during the course of a week is a knife and fork. So please be sensible and practise before a round. I am not, for one moment, suggesting that you now get to the club three hours before your game and slog away on the practice tee. There's no need for that; for one thing, after such a session you would probably be too tired to even start a round of golf. But a few shots on the practice ground with most of your clubs will pay handsome dividends. You can expect to, and will, knock as many as half a dozen shots off your score by doing this.

There is absolutely no excuse for missing a tee shot. Technically it's the easiest shot in the game, and if you think about it, you'll agree. You always hit the ball off a wooden tee peg so there is no bad lie, thick rough or any such problem to interfere with the swing. Here now is the ideal situation to go ahead and execute the golf swing in the manner in which I have just described it.

The object of the driver is to propel that ball as far as possible, to a position on the fairway which will set you up for your next shot, and in most cases, if you have done the job properly, you will be aiming for the green. Unfortunately far too many club golfers change their personalities as soon as they step onto the tee. From the moment they take the driver in their hands they become power crazy, they have but one desire, to hit that ball with everything they've got. This invariably sets into motion a disastrous chain of events. They swing back too quickly, destroying their rhythm and ruining their timing. Now having lost their control, they hit wildly at the ball with little, if any, accuracy. If luck's with them the ball lands on the fairway, but the odds are it will finish up somewhere in the rough. This is both pointless and silly, for when you put your tee shot into the rough, a bunker or any such hazard, you are facing two problems: getting out of the trouble is one of them—trying to reach the green the other. The golden rule to remember when you step onto the tee obsessed with the thought of driving the ball out of sight is this:

> If you want to hit it farther
> Don't try to hit it harder
> Try to hit it better.

So steady now, let's have a nice controlled swing. Don't worry if it means sacrificing a little length, make sure you get the ball on the fairway, then all you have to worry about is hitting that ball on the green. Perhaps it will help you if I illustrate some tee tips of my own, which I have used successfully in many tournaments.

If there is a lot of trouble on the left-hand side of the fairway, tee the ball *low*. There is very little loft on the driver and even top professionals find it difficult to hook a ball off the fairway with this club because of the lack of loft on the face. So tee it low and the result will be a shot which has, if anything, a slight fade to the right.

If you have trouble on the right-hand side of the fairway then tee the ball higher. Do not be afraid to aim slightly down the right-hand side of the fairway, in fact this will help the shot. Now swing freely back, slightly inside the line of flight, with a really good

(a) If there's trouble on the left side of the fairway I always tee down. With a low tee the tendency is to slice

(b) But if the trouble is on the right I find it better to tee up. With a high tee you invariably get a draw

(c) But if you want to hit one down the middle I find it's best to place the tee-peg between my first two fingers and just allow the grass to brush them. This way the ball is about an inch off the grass, the ideal position. Using this method you can be sure your tee height will never vary

(a) If you are looking for extra length off the tee develop the two power points of the swing

(b) When the club comes down into the hitting area concentrate all the power of the swing into the trigger finger of the right hand

(c) At the same time kick off with the right foot. The kick throws your weight right through the ball, giving you tremendous clubhead speed and forcing you into a nice high follow through—the postscript to a really powerful swing shoulder turn and hit past the chin. It will help the shot if you stay back a bit on the right leg at impact.

For the straightforward tee shot on a nice wide open fairway, I always put the tee-peg between my first two fingers and push it into the ground until my fingers brush the grass. This ensures that the ball will stand about an inch off the grass. I strongly recommend you adopt this method for then you will be sure that the ball will be teed at the same height every time. An important feature of a golf pro's game is uniformity and consistency in *all* things, teeing the ball to the correct height is just one of them.

Finally if you are having trouble finding the fairway with your driver, don't be too proud to change to a No. 2 wood. After all, Peter Thomson and Bobby Locke both won Open championships driving with lofted woods. If they felt justified in adopting this measure there's no reason why you shouldn't. Take my advice, give it a try until the time comes when you regain your lost confidence in the driver.

TAKE A TIP . . .

You will rarely flavour the excitement of an extra long tee shot if you merely try to hit the ball—You must aim to accelerate through it.

5

FAIRWAY WOODS

Never be afraid to use a wood off the fairway provided the ball
has a reasonable lie. If the ball is sitting up nicely on the grass take
the No. 2 wood, but if there are any doubts in your mind, a more
lofted wood like a No. 3, or possibly a No. 4.

Most club golfers demand one thing from a fairway wood—
distance. An admirable thought, providing they don't get over-
ambitious. They must fight against the temptation to speed up,
overswing and so lose balance as they strive for the extra power to
hit the ball harder. The end result is usually a long and unprofitable
search in the rough for a ball of which they were once the proud
owner. Try to picture you are sweeping the ball away rather than
striking it a definite blow. Over the years I have found the best
way of making this sweep work is to imagine you have four balls
in a line pointing towards the hole, the one you are going to hit
and three more placed in front of it. The object is to sweep
through the first ball and continue through all four, one after the
other. This exercise prevents you from chopping down sharply
at the ball and helps you to achieve a smooth, sweeping swing.

I have also found the four wood a mighty good friend when my
ball is in fairly heavy rough. In most cases the four wood can get

Sweep the ball away. Imagine you have four balls in a line pointing towards the hole

your ball out a lot better than, say, an eight or nine iron. As long as you can take the club back fairly smoothly through the rough, and there's no immediate trouble in front of you, such as bunkers, go ahead and use it. For this shot, grip well down the shaft and swing firmly but easily. A wooden headed club will go right through the grass, spreading it without cutting it. Not so with an iron,

A 4 wood can be used from the rough with excellent results. It will spread the grass and not get tangled in it like an iron

the blade will tear through the grass which tangles round the clubhead, reducing it's speed. In many cases this shuts the clubface and the ball goes nowhere. But even if you slightly mis-hit it with a wood, you will still get a reasonable shot with plenty of roll.

Let's take another situation. . . . You are playing into the wind, have a reasonable lie and there is no trouble between you and the green. What club do you use? I say a *driver*. Yes, even if you're not very good at it. Should you half top this shot, you'll keep it under the wind and it'll go something like 200 yards. A ball is round and it will run, that's what it is meant to do. Most golfers feel ashamed when they catch a ball thin and it hardly gets up into the air. They sense failure as it spends the best part of its journey racing along the ground towards the green. Why? There's nothing wrong with that. It's a perfectly good shot. Let's take it a stage further. We all accept we can't pitch a ball onto a bone-hard green and expect it to hold. So we pitch it well short

Aim to hit the top half of the ball when using a driver from the fairway into a strong wind

WIND

and watch it roll over the fairway, across the green and up to the flag. We accept this as a good stroke because it was intentional—we disown the thinned fairway shot, even though it was successful —because it was unintentional. This is weak thinking—you were aiming for the green and that's where it went, the route it took is not important, don't be too air conscious and accept good luck as well as bad. Tony Cerda almost specialised in thin straight ones. People used to say to him 'Oh, what a lucky shot' or 'That wasn't a very good one' and he would laugh and reply 'Ah, señor, but it is on the green, not in the bushes!' *The straight, thin one is the best bad shot in golf—remember that.*

TAKE A TIP . . .

When a club player makes an excellent stroke, he beams with delight and then talks about it to his opponent. He never gives a thought as to how he did it. Usually when a player makes a really bad stroke, he goes through the motions of playing it again. Far better to adopt this procedure after your exceptional stroke, you will learn more.

With your long irons a three-quarter backswing is all
that is required. But a full turn of the shoulders must
accompany this

6

THE LONG IRONS

A two iron off the fairway is one of the most difficult shots there is in golf, like the driver, it has very little loft, but unlike the driver, you have no tee peg to help you. It takes a lot of time and practice to be able to handle this club with confidence. But when mastered the rewards are great.

The reason the average golfer finds the two and three iron so difficult is because the face of the club is so very small and straight. You must hit the ball dead in the centre of the clubface to produce a long accurate shot, should you hit it slightly on the toe or heel, it will dribble off nowhere. There is not the margin of error with these clubs that there is with the four wood. The large clubface of the wood is almost twice that of the two or three iron. That is why the average golfer is so much more confident with it. He knows that if he doesn't catch it smack in the middle of the clubface he will still get a reasonably good shot. Many of our top professionals prefer to use a four or even a five wood to the dreaded straight-faced long iron. And why not? They know the advantages the wood offers, and so they use it. Copy them if you are having trouble with your long irons, or read on and I will show you the correct way to master these clubs.

E.G.—D

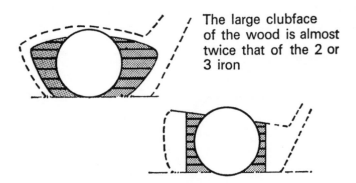

The large clubface of the wood is almost twice that of the 2 or 3 iron

Again, on the long irons you must visualise the shot as a *sweep* rather than a definite hit. Agreed, all iron shots must be struck with a descending blow, but don't think this means taking an extra large divot. Your aim is to hit a descending blow which just clips the grass—nothing more.

We have a slightly narrower stance with the irons, to compensate for the slightly shorter club lengths, but remember the 'magic triangle', don't move the position of the ball, keep it in line with the left heel. Your body weight, if anything, should tend to favour your left side. Assuming a square stance, flex your knees slightly and hold your head up. As I explained before it is wrong to tuck it into your chest like a tortoise.

Break the wrists fairly early in the backswing, but remember to keep the first two feet of the take-away smooth and easy. After that you can accelerate as much as you like, as long as you build up the speed gradually without destroying your rhythm.

Maintain the same pressure of grip throughout the swing, do not re-grip or tense up, especially at impact. This is a fatal error which will ruin the shot.

A three-quarter backswing is all that is required, but a full turn of the shoulders must accompany this.

From the top of the backswing, the first movement is the turning of the left hip, followed by the left shoulder, left arm and last of all the hands.

Concentrate on a good rhythmic swing and sweep through the ball, have the confidence to let the clubhead do the work for you. As you sweep through the ball keep the right arm extended and pointing to the target as long as possible. Then, when your club gets parallel to the ground, the natural force of the swing will pull your head up.

Maintain your balance as your hands travel up into a nice high finish. A word of caution—with the long irons, play it safe, always aim for the biggest part of the green, so that you will have the widest possible margin of error.

A useful tip. Don't always think in terms of a 'big' shot with the two or three irons. I have found it can be employed very successfully when you are faced with a chip shot to the green which has to be kept low to avoid overhanging branches. Remember there will be quite a considerable amount of roll on this sort of shot, so make allowances for it.

A 2 or 3 iron can be used very successfully when faced with a chip shot which has to be kept low

TAKE A TIP . . .

The farther a golfer swings back for extra power, the more he increases his chances of error. The end result is usually an out-of-control swing, followed by an out-of-bounds ball.

7

THE MEDIUM IRONS

With the middle irons, the four, five and six, we are looking to play a shot which will put us on the green and enable us to get down in two more. All golfers find that they can play these shorter irons with both confidence and authority. This is because the swing is more compact, which means you have more control over the execution of the shot.

Because of the shortness in shaft you are moving even closer to the ball. This means a more upright swing, so it becomes very difficult to play a sweeping shot. But here again, it is not necessary to take a big divot. The feet are a little closer together and the ball is still played from off the left heel. A good tip here I find is to line up to the target with the bottom of the blade and not the top as this tends to close the clubface. For these middle irons we need nothing more than a three-quarter backswing with the arms and hands controlling the whole movement. The distribution of your weight should now definitely favour your left side. A word of warning . . . because this is a simple, easy swing, there is a tendency to ease up at impact. This is wrong, hit the shot with great authority and let the arms take the club to a good full follow-through.

Never, I repeat, never, *press* with these irons. If you think that you can get to a green with a seven iron, but know to do so will mean striving for maximum power, don't attempt it. You are bound to lose some accuracy and may well knock the ball into trouble. Take a six iron and swing well within yourself. All the great players—Palmer, Nicklaus, Player and company—play well within themselves on all shots from within 120 yards radius of the green.

With the middle irons you should make sure that you play away from trouble; plan these shots with great care, for this is the time when strokes are saved or lost. We are aiming for the green but we are also making sure we avoid traps and greenside trouble. Having selected the safest route to the flag, don't be greedy, do aim for the biggest part of the green. It is foolish to try to get the ball close to the flag in the hope of a one-putt and in doing so stand a chance, if your ball is slightly off line, of landing in trouble, and dropping two or even three strokes at one hole.

In this case I can't agree with the old adage *'never up—never in'*. On the majority of courses that I've played, all the trouble's been at the back of the green. So play it short and let it roll up onto the green. Better to finish with a putt, even it it's a fairly long one, than to go through the green and find yourself in some thick rough which means a difficult chip back. I have also noted that the golfer who looks once at the green often needs two to get on, but the player who looks twice generally gets on in one—the morale . . . *think before you play.*

These medium irons can also be used very successfully as chipping clubs. The four, five and six all have enough loft to get that ball up into the air and send it rolling towards the flag. These simple low-flying chips can be stroke savers in windy conditions.

TAKE A TIP . . .

Analyse each round of golf you play. For instance, if you are in the habit of falling short on approach shots and so finding trouble, make a note to use more club in future.

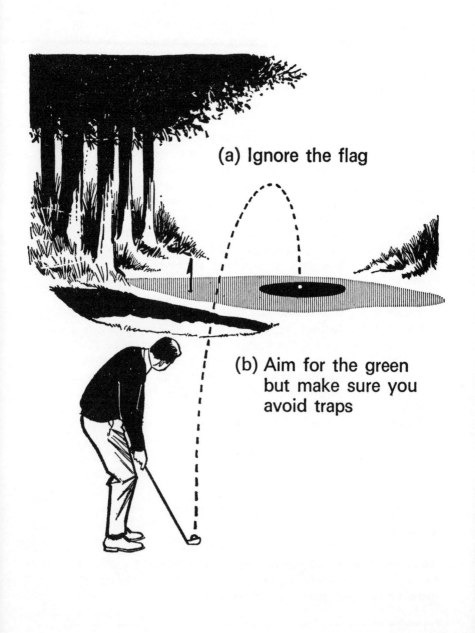

(a) Ignore the flag

(b) Aim for the green but make sure you avoid traps

I don't agree with the old adage 'never up—never in'

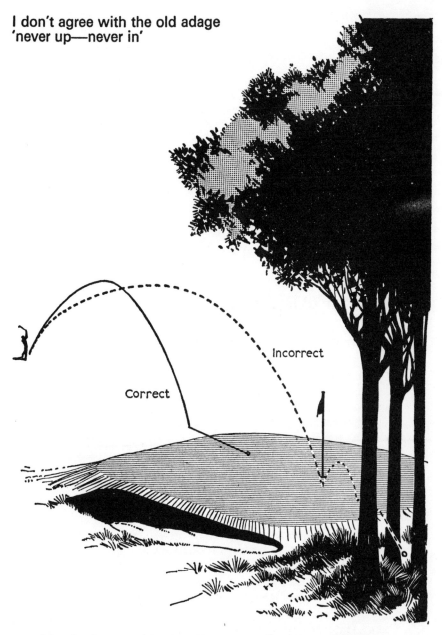

Correct

Incorrect

Play it short and let it roll up onto the green. Better to finish with a long putt than to go through the green and find yourself in trouble

8

THE SHORT IRONS

All shots within 100 yards' radius of the green call for great accuracy, no great power is needed from this close range. The seven, eight, nine and ten irons are the clubs we figure on using, but not always. If you can put the ball near the flag with a two iron or even a putter, use it. The best method is obviously the one that gets the ball closest to the flag, we are looking for a one-putt, or at worst two. These shots of 100 yards or less call for many half and three-quarter swings. The decision is one the golfer must make for himself. For example, one player may use a half swing with a seven iron and another, from the same distance, use a three-quarter swing with an eight iron. These shots are played mainly with the arms, with the feet quite close together. You are standing very near the ball now, so your swing will be almost upright. A nice, easy rhythm with a firm hit and good follow-through is all that is required.

Again the choice of clubs is not governed by distance alone—these shots require careful thought—too many club golfers simply hit the ball towards the green and leave it to solve its own problems. If it lands in trouble they curse their bad luck. If it makes the green they are delighted, they have asked no more from the shot.

This is wrong, they should have been aiming at the green with a definite chance of getting up there near the flag. A simple check to see if the flag was at the front or back of the green, the position of the bunkers, if the ground slopes towards the green and so on, would have greatly increased their chance of success. They may have succeeded with a different choice of club or by aiming in a

Try bowling a ball underarm to the flag to capture the feeling of a correctly played chip shot

different direction—but this they will never know because they didn't stop to think.

More shots are fluffed when golfers find themselves just off the green than anywhere else on the course. They either pitch up well short of the flag or send it miles past. For this sort of chip shot I suggest you start practising without a club. Try bowling the ball underarm to the flag. Your eye will tell you where you should pitch the ball onto the green so that it will roll the necessary distance to the flag. Using a smooth, underarm swing, release the ball and let ynor arm follow down the line to the hole. Do this a couple of dozen times and you will be surprised how near you will be able to get that ball to the hole. Having satisfied yourself how easy it is, take a club and imagine that the clubface is your right hand. Now take that club back, swing it down and bowl that ball up to the flag. It's as simple as that.

This shot is played almost entirely with the arms—so remember, head still, hands well down the shaft, knees bent and feet almost together. Now simply swing the arms back, down and through to the target—a tight controlled swing with a firm hit.

Here again, I don't think it matters what club you use when playing these short chips from just off the green. You may feel happiest with a putter, a two iron or even a wedge. South African Bobby Locke always used his wedge for chipping, even when on the very edge of the green. This club suited Locke, and he won tournament after tournament with it. So who is to say this method is wrong? Charlie Ward, a great exponent of the short game, used two clubs, a four iron and a wedge, always pitching the ball on to the green.

When chipping from the rough around the green a *chopping down* stroke is required, no bowling action here. I suggest you use a wedge or sand iron, open the blade of the club slightly and grip down the shaft. Grass has a habit of catching round the neck of the club and

When chipping from the rough around the green, a chopping-down action is required

Incorrect   Correct

shutting the face, so direct the blade at the ball. Once again, a narrow stance and remember everything in this shot must be firm, tightly controlled and positive. On the backswing take your hands back to at least, hip height, then swing down firmly at that ball and *no quitting* on the shot.

Don't think you have to be on the green before you take the putter from the bag. You can be just as successful putting off the green as on it. Remember the putt is the simplest shot in the bag to play and the easiest to control. This is the shot us pros call the 'Texas wedge'. But this I must stress—never consider this method unless the conditions are suitable. If there is thick grass between the ball and the green, forget it. Also, if the ground in front of the green is very bumpy, it could prove to be too risky a stroke. But once you have decided to play this shot you can be sure of one thing—it will never get you into any serious trouble. It may run a little off line, it may finish past the cup or short of it, but at least you have achieved your object—you are on the green. There is little chance of you topping or hitting behind the ball with a putter.

From experience I have found that the golfer who can chip well is the one who hits his long iron shots to the green with the greatest confidence. He knows that if he should miss the green he can rectify matters by playing a good chip close to the hole.

TAKE A TIP . . .

The sole purpose of short irons is that of accuracy and not distance. Too many golfers ruin their approach shots by demanding both. A good way to cure yourself of this power complex is to think in terms of hitting the flag rather than hitting the ball.

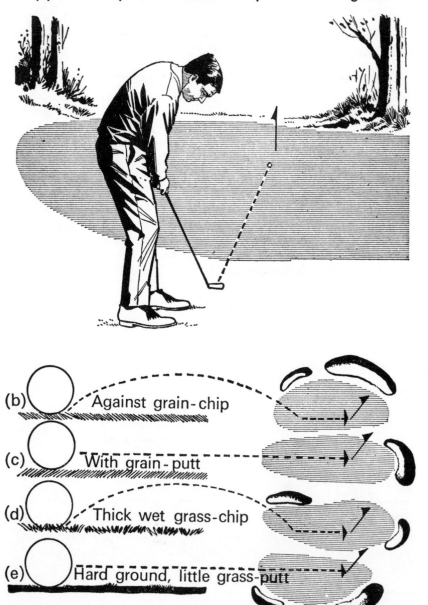

(a) When to putt and when to chip from off the green

(b) Against grain-chip

(c) With grain-putt

(d) Thick wet grass-chip

(e) Hard ground, little grass-putt

9

THE WEDGE

We are told the wedge was originally invented by an american named Eugene Saraceni, better known today as Gene Sarazen—a name he adopted because he thought his own sounded too much like a violin player. By adding thick lumps of solder to the underside of his niblick, Sarazen made a club which he could use successfully in sand bunkers. Until then he had lost many tournaments as a direct result of bad bunker play. Sarazen's brain child was born the day he stopped to watch a plane. He noticed the tail went down as the nose went up at take-off. So Gene reasoned that by adding extra weight to the sole or tail of his niblick the face of the club would come up as the sole went down and made contact with the sand. Smart thinking which paid off for Sarazen. He became a master bunker player and consistent championship winner.

But no longer is the wedge just used for bunker play, today it has become an all-purpose club. Because of it's heavy sole and lofted blade, it is ideal for sending the ball high in the air and dropping it almost vertical at the pin. This club can be used for hitting to the green form any distance up to 100 yards. But at no time should it be swung with full power. It is used essentially for accuracy and

(a) Place your feet fairly close together and just swing with the arms

(b) The wedge is the ideal club when it calls for a shot with a high loft and a quick stop therefore it is played with a three-quarter swing or less. Once again very little body movement is used in the stroke. Place your feet almost together and just swing with the arms, nice easy rhythm, firm hit and good follow-through. Many club golfers fluff this shot by trying to use their hands to give the ball added loft. *Don't scoop*—have confidence in the loft on the clubface. Simply hit down and through, keeping your head still. I repeat—*hit down to hit up.*

The sole purpose of the wedge is to get the ball up into the air quickly and stop it quickly when it lands. Practise with this club and master it for it can save you many, many strokes, but do not become a slave to it. Study your route to the green carefully, then, if it calls for a shot with a high loft and a quick stop (possibly a bunker between you and the green) use a wedge. But if it is trouble-free between you and the green, play a simple pitch and run with one of the short irons; the safest route is always the best route for getting your ball to the flag.

It may not always be the best looking shot which gets the best results; sometimes a less spectacular shot, even one which travels all along the ground, gets the best reward. As I have said before the greatest single mistake I find among handicap golfers is that they tend to forget they are playing with a round ball and that all round objects have a tendency to roll. They are too obsessed with playing all their shots in the air. Ask yourself if you are guilty of this—if you are then you are playing golf the hard way—and possibly dropping strokes in the process.

TAKE A TIP . . .

In their eagerness to see their wedge shot hit the green, too many golfers look up and commit the sin of lifting their head and so ruin a perfectly good shot. An excellent way to avoid this is to listen for the sound of the blade hitting the ball. This will ensure your head stays down until the ball is well on it's way.

10

PUTTING

You don't get many tall players who are good putters. In fact you don't get many tall people who are good golfers. Most of the world's greats have been under six feet. Men such as Player, Nicklaus, Palmer, Hogan, Jones, Vardon, Cotton, Locke, Hagen and Sarazen prove this. I think the reason for this is that a tall man is too far away from the ball. The higher up you are the more things have to move, the shoulders, hips, legs—everything is so much more exaggerated. Also their swing radius—left shoulder to clubhead—is longer, which means a bigger and more difficult swing arc to control. I honestly think if I'd been two inches shorter, say 5 ft. 11 in., I would have been a far better golfer than I am now. This goes for putting as well; a short man is right down there with his eye on the ball, he's much more compact and so naturally has more control. Possibly that's why when you give a small boy a putter he swings away merrily, popping them in the hole, one after another. . . . No problems.

Personally I have gained a false reputation for being a bad putter, mainly due to my own doing. I've joked too much about it and talked too much about it. Now I'm not saying I'm a great putter, I'm not, but, by the same yardstick, I'm certainly not the world's worst. I've played rounds where I've sunk two or three long putts. By long putts I mean something over forty feet, but during that same round I may have missed two of say three feet. Now you can be sure there were many newspapers, magazines and what have you, which didn't mention the long putts, they simply said, 'Alliss came in with a seventy-two but it should have been so much better—he missed two simple three-foot putts.' Throughout my career it's always been the case of people remembering the short putts I've missed and forgetting the long ones I've holed.

I know, only too well, thanks to my putting reputation, that every golf club has got a champion putter, at least the ones I've been to have. I meet them every weekend when I play exhibition matches. People come up to me and say, 'You want to see old Bert, he bangs them in from all over the place. If only you could putt like him, you'd be a world beater!' But I could putt old Bert every day of the week for £1,000 a hole and beat him every time. If I putted Casper for £1,000 a hole he'd beat me many times, although I'd still beat him occasionally, but I'd beat old Bert every time. The reason old Bert is a good putter in his own circle is because he's not subjected to any pressures. I'm used to putting for money so the cash wouldn't worry me—but not so old Bert, the thought of it would turn him and his putter white with fright!

So don't be misled into thinking every time a golfer misses a crucial but seemingly simple putt in a big tournament that the occasion has proved too much and his nerves have betrayed him. We professionals have to master this nervous strain, we have to live with it and I don't think it unduly affects our scoring. As you know yourself, in a friendly game with one of your friends, you can miss a three or even a two foot putt and there is no tension or nerves playing a part there. It's purely and simply a human error.

There is not a golfer living who hasn't made a mistake on the greens—it is easy to be tricked by it's gentle slopes and subtle textures. But for all that there is one thing we can be sure of, as long as we live we'll never find a hole that will come and meet the ball, the ball must go to the hole. The player who misses his putts by going past the hole is an infinitely better putter than the one who misses his by always being short. The man who's always finishing six inches short very seldom three-putts, but then he

E.G.—E

will hardly, if ever, one-putt. Whereas the player who is always
going past gets a great number of single putts. Agreed, he may
also get a couple of three's, but if you don't get your share of one-
putt's, you're not going to break seventy very often. One of the
greatest putters of our time is undoubtedly Arnold Palmer. He
always tries for the hole and it's an event if, during a round, a
couple of his putts die before reaching the hole. I think Doug Ford,
a great putter, summed this up superbly when he said 'I was never
short with my first, second, third, fourth or fifth putt!'

Talking about positive putters reminds me of Bobby Locke.
Bobby used to hook everything, even his putts. Time after time
the ball would drop in the hole on the right-hand side of the cup.
But he was truly a great putter, one of the greatest of all time. I've
never seen anybody more confident on the green than him.

If nothing frightened Locke on the greens, nothing ever hurried
him either. . . . And quite right too. Now there is a very good reason
for all this so-called time wasting which some people say we pros
do when on the putting surface. The walking up and down the line
of the putt, picking up imaginary bits of stuff, looking at it from
the front, looking at it from the back, lining it up. These are the
actions which give us the time we need to get absolutely ready to
hit the shot. It's a cleansing of the mind; you must be rid of any
thoughts which are not related to striking that ball. You'd be
surprised how quickly your mind can wander and so ruin your
concentration. Possibly an unusual coloured jumper around the
gallery will catch your eye, you might even find yourself thinking
about your next tee shot. Until his mind is free of these distractions
no tournament golfer will strike his putt. I'm not suggesting that
every club golfer goes through a three-act pantomime on the
green, just remember—*Don't strike the putt until you are ready*.

Then when you are ready, don't be afraid to hit it firmly. All the
great putters, Bobby Locke, Billy Casper, Arnold Palmer, and
Gary Player, strike the ball hard—they also have another thing
in common, they come from countries where the greens are nearly
always bad. It makes me shudder when I think of some of the
rough and bumpy ones in South Africa, where you must strike the
ball hard and true to have any hope of getting the ball in the hole.
So it is with the courses in Florida; they have Bermuda grass,
where again, the strike is all important. Golfers in these lands

first learn how to strike a ball, and once you learn how to strike it, the speed and everything else falls into place. The British greens are almost too good and the ball, when mis-hit, will still roll up to the hole and trickle in. This cultivates bad habits, one must *accelerate* the clubhead during impact in putting, as indeed in all shots in golf.

Many of the great putters I know hit the ball half way up to make sure the top half of the ball moves towards the hole first and not the bottom half. This, of course, was one of Bobby Locke's great secrets—firmly striking the top half of the ball and getting it rolling forward, hugging the ground.

There are hundreds of different putting styles, just as many different shapes of putters and an even greater variety of grips that golfers use on them. What is the best method, the right grip? Who really knows? The one which gets the ball in the hole is the one I advise you to use, even if it means holding your putter upside down. But if the style and method are not important, there are certain proven facts which must be obeyed if you want to putt well.

Firstly, when putting on very fast greens I strongly advise you to use a medium to lightweight putter. On soft, slow greens, possibly after rain, use a fairly heavy putter—you'll need it. Remember *all* shots in golf have to be struck with authority and the putt even more so. Because this is such a gentle shot, the timing has to be absolutely correct, so see to it that the clubhead is travelling quicker at impact than at any other time in the swing.

Always have a good close look at the green before you consider anything else when putting. If, on a sunny day, you see that it is light and shiny, it means that the grain of the grass is growing away from you. But if it has a dull darkish look, it means that the grain is growing towards you. Remember, when it grows towards you strike the ball a little harder than you think necessary, and when it's growing towards the hole, it doesn't require such a firm hit because there is no resistance from the grass.

On soft wet greens the ball seems to travel more through the grass and slopes make less impression, but if the green is hard the ball will travel on top of the grass and any slope will have a marked effect.

On fairly long putts, aim to get as close to the hole as possible;

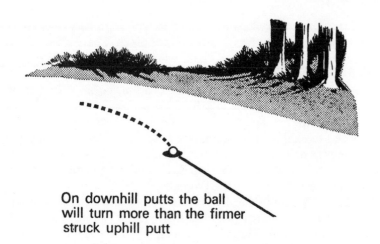

On downhill putts the ball
will turn more than the firmer
struck uphill putt

be bold, but try not to go racing past. A dying putt can fall into
the hole from four sides, but a racer has to be straight at the back
of the hole to stand any chance of dropping.

On the downhill putts the ball will turn more than the firmer
uphill putt. This is because when putting uphill you have to
strike the ball harder and therefore any borrow is minimised by
the ball's speed. But on a downhill putt we require a lighter touch
so the slope will take full effect on the slow rolling ball.

On long uphill putts consider the putt to follow. Play safe and

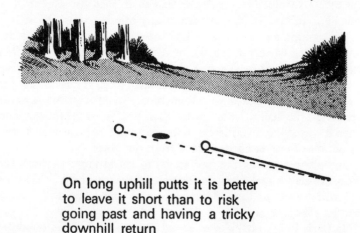

On long uphill putts it is better
to leave it short than to risk
going past and having a tricky
downhill return

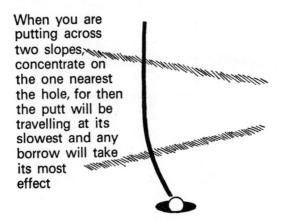

When you are putting across two slopes, concentrate on the one nearest the hole, for then the putt will be travelling at its slowest and any borrow will take its most effect

allow to err on the lower side of the hole. It's not smart thinking, if you miss, to find your return is a tricky downhill putt.

When you are putting across two slopes on the green, concentrate on the one nearest the hole, because then the putt is travelling at its slowest and any borrow will take its most effect.

On short putts that go past the hole, note the line the ball took, because this, after making the necessary adjustment, will be the correct line for the return putt.

When the grain grows in the opposite direction to a slight slope

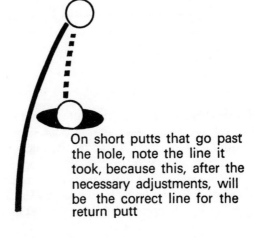

On short putts that go past the hole, note the line it took, because this, after the necessary adjustments, will be the correct line for the return putt

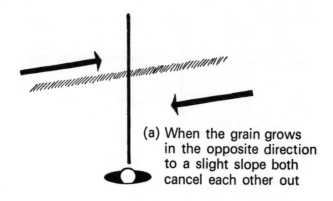

(a) When the grain grows in the opposite direction to a slight slope both cancel each other out

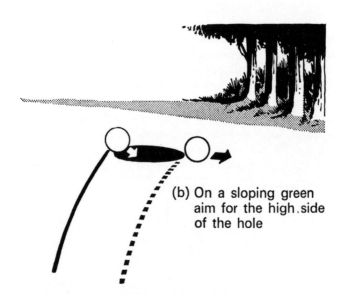

(b) On a sloping green aim for the high side of the hole

both cancel each other out, the ball will run straight.

Putt off the toe for fast putts, heel for slow putts.

Finally, once having decided on the line and strength of putt, never change your mind during the swing. Have confidence in your putting and hit the ball firmly. You'll be surprised how many of them drop in the hole. Most club golfers only half expect to sink those extra long putts of forty feet and more. So they invariably only half hit the thing and leave it woefully short. Once you have decided on the line concentrate on getting the ball up to the hole, it won't roll by itself it's got to be hit and hit hard—remember, a putt dead on line but eight feet short helps no one. But one, right up there alongside the hole—even if you have misread the line by as much as two feet—means you are left with a fairly simple tap-in.

TAKE A TIP . . .

On the putting green, under certain circumstances, you should try for no more than to get down in two putts. Even if you are only five feet from the hole, e.g. five feet above the flag at the eleventh at St. Andrews when the green is exceptionally fast.

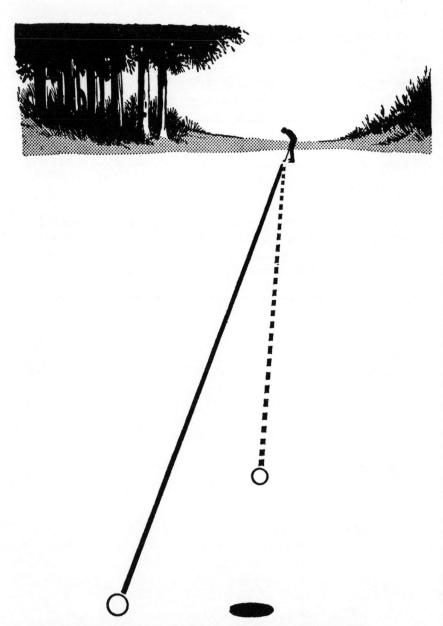

A putt, dead on line but 8 feet short, helps no-one.
But one, right up there alongside the hole—even if you
have misread the line by as much as two feet, means
that you are left with a fairly simple tap-in

11

BUNKER SHOTS

It is generally very easy to pick out the bad bunker players at any golf club, they are usually attired in sand trap white. How infuriating it must be for these golfers to be continually told by people who should know better, that these are the simplest shots in golf.

This is so much rubbish. To the first-class professionals and amateurs they *are* relatively easy shots—but I could give you a list of several top pros who are none too clever in green side bunkers. Arnold Palmer, for instance, is not in the same class as, say, Sam Snead or Gary Player.

Getting out of a bunker is simple enough but dropping that ball in a one-putt position is not at all easy. With bunker shots you face two problems, getting out is one, getting near the pin the other. So naturally many players are caught in two minds. If they take too much sand they'll end up just flopping the ball out—if they take too little they send the ball right over the green. Faced with these two possibilities, the weekender fears the worst and panics. The bold one takes a hurried backswing then slams the clubhead down into the sand. If he's lucky, the ball just flops out but the chances are he's buried it completely—the not so-bold golfer flicks the clubhead at the ball trying to pick it off the sand. Once again this sort of approach will only succeed if luck takes a hand.

How the bunker shot gained the reputation of being the simplest stroke in golf defies me. Admittedly in most cases it is the only one where you don't even have to hit the ball. It's the build-up of sand between clubface and ball which actually forces the ball out. But even so it requires a high degree of skill to take just the right amount of sand to make that ball behave as you want it.

The first thing I do when I step into a bunker is to sink my feet into the sand. Not only does this provide me with a firm footing, it also tells me the texture and composition of the sand. If it is heavy, coarse or damp, I won't take a sand wedge with a big wide sole. I prefer a pitching wedge which has a sharper leading edge and will cut into the sand and get nicely underneath the ball. Deep powdery sand calls for a heavy bunker iron with a wide sole. Such a club will almost play the shot for you. Using a nice easy swing, simply drive the clubhead down into the sand behind the ball. This creates a little explosion, the sand mounts up the clubface and pops the ball out. Once you have decided on the club best suited to the sand, make sure you grip down the shaft—this will give you greater control over the shot.

For bunker shots on a level lie you need an open stance, that is right foot slightly in front of left. You are now aiming just a little left of target; by opening the clubface slightly you keep the blade pointing to the flag. See to it that the ball is well forward, approximately in line with your left instep. Now swing out slightly across the line on the backswing. In other words, swing along the line of the feet. From the illustration you will see I have quite a considerable backswing—please copy. On the downswing we come back across the line and hit the sand an inch behind the ball, don't quit on the shot—let the arms travel through to a nice high finish. Think of it as a full swing in slow motion and the ball will come out quite easily.

To improve your accuracy at hitting the sand first and then the ball, practise this way. Draw a line behind the ball with your sand iron—now forget the ball and aim at that line. Practise this for thirty minutes or so and you will become quite an expert at popping the ball out.

(a) For bunker shots on a level lie, adopt an open stance, then swing out slightly across the target line on the backswing. In other words, swing along the line of the feet.

(b) On the downswing, come back across the target line and hit the sand an inch behind the ball—don't quit on the shot

Having dealt with the basic bunker shot, let's move on to some typical sand trap problems.

Problem: Ball at front of bunker on a steep uphill lie.
On an uphill lie you must hit the sand closer to the ball than you would on the flat. The reason for this is because the sand is that much deeper at the point of entry, which means your clubhead will travel through deeper and deeper sand as it moves upwards and through underneath the ball. This, of course, will slow up your clubhead so I say again, don't quit on the shot, hit as hard as you can behind the ball straight into the sand. Do not attempt any follow-through, the mere fact that the clubhead enters the sand behind the ball will be enough to build up sufficient sand to float the ball out onto the green. Because you are standing on an upslope it is essential to adjust your stance. To avoid swaying backwards, sink your feet in deep and keep your weight on your left side throughout the shot. Here, as before, the clubface should be kept open and square to the line of flight. Now keeping your body perfectly still swing out across the line, taking your hands up to shoulder height—then on the downswing come back across the line and hit the sand really close to the ball.

Problem: Ball at back of bunker on a steep downhill lie.
This is the problem I have just described but in reverse. On a downhill lie the depth of the sand decreases from the point where the clubhead enters. So this time we aim for a spot in the sand further behind the ball than we would for a sand shot on a normal level lie. On a downslope your left foot is lower than your right, so to avoid falling into the shot keep your weight on your right foot throughout the swing. Here again, open the clubface and swing out across the line then down and in. Because this is a downhill shot the chances are you will get little loft—so allow for it.

Problem: Ball on level lie in firm sand with no overhanging lip to bunker.
My advice here is to take your putter. Play your normal putting stroke and strike the ball dead centre. A word of caution here—

don't strike the ball above centre or you will only succeed in driving it forward into the sand—also don't hit it below centre for the chances are you will loft it a few feet and it will drop down again into the sand. So I repeat, hit it dead centre and keep it rolling along the top of the sand. This, of course, is why it is such a successful shot on hard damp sand—and why it should never be attempted in sand of a soft powdery texture.

Problem: Ball buried in deep sand.

A little tip I was told by Chi Chi Rodriguez can help us here. For a badly buried ball he told me to open the blade of the wedge, whereas most golf teachers say you should hood it. Admittedly this does get the ball out but it tends to run a lot. By opening the blade you make the leading edge of the clubface even sharper, which, of course, helps it to dig quickly and deeply into the sand. This shot calls for an exaggerated open stance—and get your feet dug well in. Now we need a nice high backswing, as upright as possible, then, exerting your maximum force, drive that clubhead in right behind the ball. Try to maintain the feeling that the blade is going deeper and deeper into the sand. There is no follow-through here, just dig in as deep as possible. The time to stop is when you can't go any further. It is amazing how easily the ball will come out and in most cases it will even have a little backspin—a good tip and one I have used with great success over the past two years.

Problem: Ball lying on top of sand in fairway bunker, 180 yards from the green.

If you want to hit the ball a long way from out of a bunker don't hit the sand first—it must be picked off cleanly. It is for this reason that the ball must be sitting up prominently. If it is fairly deep in the sand take a more lofted club and settle for less distance. But in this case, having satisfied yourself that the ball is sitting up nicely take a long iron or even a four wood—now keep your eyes fixed on the ball and swing easily. Remember, you are standing in loose sand and this can play tricks with your foothold. So get those feet firmly anchored. I say again, make sure you hit the ball first and not the sand behind it. Don't, of course, quit on the shot and do finish with a nice high follow-through.

(a) For a badly buried ball adopt an exaggerated open stance

(b) Open the blade of the wedge

(c) A nice high backswing, as upright as possible

(d) Drive clubhead into the sand right behind the ball ... there is no follow through

Bunker shots are important, we all, at one time or another, find ourselves in one, so please spend a little time practising them. Sam Snead told me, if he could go back twenty-five years he would only practise driving, putting and *bunker shots*.

TAKE A TIP . . .

The first concern of the weekend golfer, when he finds himself in a sand trap just off the green, should be to get out. He must save his miracles for the green.

Always study the contours of the green and make them work for you—not against

12

PLAYING THE COURSE

To play a round of golf is easy—it's playing it well that's hard.
One way of planning a round is to pace off distances from certain
landmarks on the course to the centre of the green. The landmarks
can be trees, bushes, posts, just about anything as long as it's a
permanent fixture. Jack Nicklaus once paced out a course using
the trash cans as landmarks—unfortunately for Jack, somebody
shifted the cans into different positions, which meant, of course,
he had to do the job all over again. Just what club you will need to
hit a ball, say, 150 of your paces is something you will have to
work out for yourself on the practice ground. But for this work
you will be well rewarded, for it is then a simple matter of checking
the landmark from where your ball lies to the green. If it is 140
paces, you know from all that hard work on the practice ground
this is, for you, an easy six iron. Now the guess work has gone out
of your game, watch your scores come down.

When you step onto the tee take a good look where all the trouble
lies. Now tee up on the side closest to that trouble—this means
you will now be hitting away from it. Don't fall into the trap that
so many high handicap golfers do, of teeing up as far away from
the trouble as possible. They finish up pointing towards the

trouble and promptly end up despatching their ball there.

On the shorter-distance par three holes where you can take an iron, always use a tee peg. By teeing it up you are certain of hitting the ball first and this means increased backspin. This comes in very useful when you want your ball to stay put on a small green. A word of warning—these holes may be short but it doesn't necessarily mean they are simple. Treat them with respect or you'll end up taking a four or even a six.

When you find your ball deep in heavy rough it is not a time to panic or get greedy—this is no place to go looking for miracles. Forget distance and simply try to get out. If your first attempt is unsuccessful and you only manage to move the ball a few feet— stop and think. Agreed you are still in the rough, so your problem hasn't altered—but your ball's position has—take a closer look at it, you may be able to use a different club now. Don't get mad and try to smash the ball out—your score card will quickly prove you can't. Use a controlled swing, please—you'll get out, I promise you, I honestly can't think of a golfer who went into the rough and was never seen again.

When faced with an elevated green take a longer club than the one you would generally use when aiming at a green the same distance when on a level fairway. The ball will not travel so far because the elevated green reduces the parabola of the shot. The problem is reversed when aiming from a high elevated position to a green below. Now the ball will travel much farther because the extra drop extends the parabola of the shot. In these situations select a shorter club than the one you would use for the distance over level ground.

Don't be too ambitious when you have to play over a bunker to reach the green. The smart way is to aim for that part of the green on the far side of the hole. Then if you are short you will still be on the green and not in the bunker. Hazards like bunkers or even streams in front of a green should never intimidate you—the clubs in your bag have the range to help you miss them. Have confidence in your ability and trust your swing. Strive for more than that and you'll finish up in all sorts of trouble.

Playing a round of golf demands the best from both your mental and physical resources. Improve your concentration by planning your next shot as you walk up the fairway to where your ball rests.

Now your mind is free to check just how your ball lies. Play your golf this way and you will be surprised how much more in command you will be—no more standing around pondering the situation—a practice which wastes time and bores your partner.

It's a mistake to become obsessed with the hazards on a golf course; to keep checking bunker positions and such like is negative thinking. It creates unnecessary fears and builds up tension, a combination which forces you into errors and into those very hazards you may have been planning to avoid. To do yourself justice you must think more positively. Having checked the positions of likely trouble spots, ignore them and concentrate on the pleasanter aspects of the course. Sort out those flat, even parts of the fairways, those ideal positions which allow a trouble-free route to the green. Think of these and swing freely. Make the course your friend and enjoy your golf.

TAKE A TIP . . .

Find out your danger holes. If you nearly always take eight at the twelfth, make sure you *don't*. You can do this by simply playing with a five iron from the tee or any other method whereby you can keep out of the jungle.

13

UPHILL, DOWNHILL AND SIDEHILL LIES

There is nothing more infuriating than hitting a long straight drive right down the middle of the fairway only to find you are faced with a sidehill, downhill or even uphill lie. Nobody likes to play their second shots from these positions. Admittedly this is the sort of situation which confronts the weekend golfer much more than the professionals, simply because the weekender is not able to place his drives so accurately as the pro. To play these shots correctly requires a different swing pattern than the one we use when standing on level ground. The changes are subtle ones but when incorporated into your swing you will find you can play those difficult shots with a great deal of authority.

THE DOWNHILL LIE

The fairway here slopes away from you, which means you are standing with your right foot higher than your left. Contrary to a lot of teaching I say put extra weight on your left foot. This will help you hit down and through the shot. To ensure the ball will be struck by the clubhead when it reaches the lowest part of the swing, move the ball back towards your higher right foot. Select a club with more loft than you would use from the same distance on level ground. For example, a six iron will play like a five, this is because the slope of the ground will cancel out some of the loft of the club. At address bend your right knee in slightly, this will keep your hips on a level plane. Now very little footwork is used in

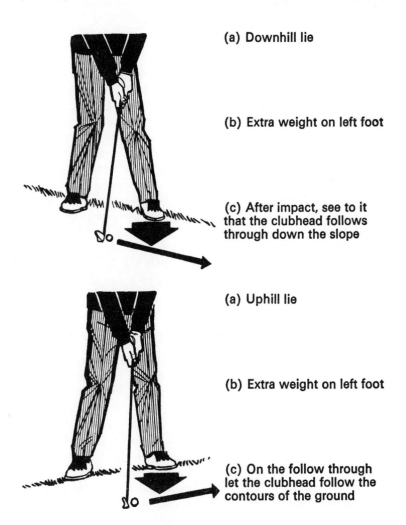

(a) Downhill lie

(b) Extra weight on left foot

(c) After impact, see to it that the clubhead follows through down the slope

(a) Uphill lie

(b) Extra weight on left foot

(c) On the follow through let the clubhead follow the contours of the ground this shot for balance is essential, so concentrate on a nice easy swing. Hit down and through the shot, and please resist the temptation to help scoop the ball up with your hands, leave it to the loft of the club to get the ball up. After impact see to it that the clubhead follows through down the slope as long as possible.

THE UPHILL LIE

Now we face the same problem in reverse. It does not matter which club you take, you will still hit the ball higher than normal, which, naturally enough, means less distance. So here again select a club with less loft than you would for the same distance on level ground. If you generally take a five iron for this shot, you will now need a four. Although, of course, if you are on an extra steep hill choose a club of two or more numbers lower. The ball position for this shot must be moved nearer the left foot to enable the clubhead to strike the ball at the bottom of the swing arc. Keep your weight on your left foot throughout the swing, gravity is always pulling you backwards, so lean into the slope. Again a nice easy swing, very little foot work is called for in this shot, balance is the key to carrying it off successfully. On the follow-through it is important to let the clubhead follow the contours of the ground, otherwise you will hit into the slope and so quit on the shot.

THE SIDEHILL LIE (BALL BELOW FEET)

Because the ball is below your feet stand a little closer to it than you would for a normal lie. To avoid reaching for the ball grip the club handle at its limit. Now flex the knees sufficiently to bring the body as near to the ball as it would be on level ground. Remember the ball will tend to go in the same direction as the ground slopes, so allow for the slice and aim to the left of the green. Once again a nice easy swing, it will be a little more upright than normal because you are standing nearer to the ball. Keep your weight on your heels, for this helps to preserve balance. Remember gravity is always pulling you into this shot. It is not too noticeable at address but it's attraction is multiplied by the force of the swing. Finally, to help ensure solid contact it is

(a) Downhill lie

(b) Ball will travel in the direction of the slope allow for it

(a) Uphill lie

(b) Ball will travel in the direction of the slope allow for it

necessary to stay down with the shot until well into the follow-through.

THE SIDEHILL LIE (BALL ABOVE FEET)

For this shot you will have to stand further away from the ball. To offset the gravitational pull, keep your weight on the balls of your feet. Grip down the shaft to compensate for the shorter swing arc. Again the ball will go in the same direction as the ground slopes so allow for the hook and aim to the right of the green. Remember you are standing further away from the ball so you will obviously have a flatter swing. Balance, as I keep saying, must be maintained so swing easy and simply play the shot with your arms and hands; very little footwork is necessary.

To play these shots successfully, don't be too ambitious with regard to length. It really is essential to have a smooth unhurried swing—get greedy and strive for distance and you will lunge at the ball, destroying your balance and end up in all sorts of trouble. Like all shots in golf, when you want to hit the ball further—concentrate on hitting it better.

TAKE A TIP . . .

In these situations avoid overswinging and be sure to take one or two practice swings before hitting the ball. This will familiarise you with the problems of weight transference.

14

PLAYING IN WINDY CONDITIONS

Think, think, think on a windy day—
If you want to keep your ball in play—

A very old saying and a very true one. When the wind blows, it's difficult even for a top professional to card a low score. It is foolhardy to attack the course in these tricky conditions. Go looking for birdies and you'll find trouble. Play sensibly and safe or the wind will blow your score sky-high. For all shots on a windy day, widen your stance. This will resist the efforts of the wind to blow you off balance.

PLAYING INTO THE WIND

You must keep the ball low and straight when playing into the wind. A hook or slice which will find the fairway on a still day will be greatly accentuated and probably end up in the rough. Even a well hit low ball will gradually rise as it battles the wind, then, when it's force is spent, it will drop almost at once. Don't expect too much roll because you won't get it, so make allowances for this fact. Depending on the strength of the wind select a stronger

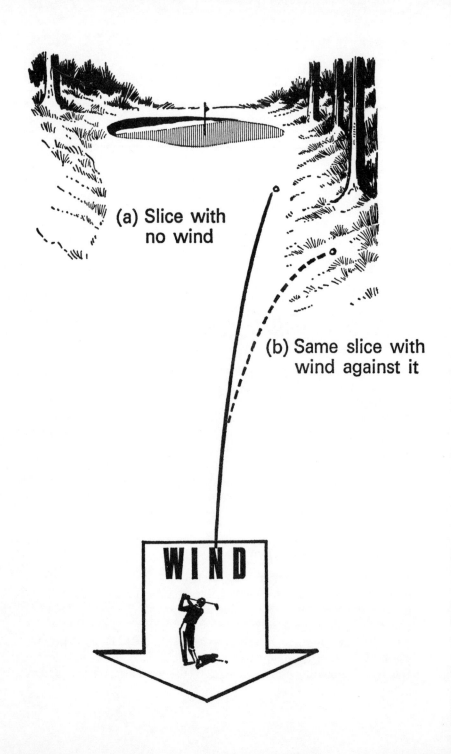

(a) Slice with no wind

(b) Same slice with wind against it

WIND

club than you would for the same distance under normal conditions. Grip two inches further down the shaft, this will narrow
your swing arc and make the whole action more compact. Hold
your hands up and in front of the ball at address; with your hands
slightly forward of the ball you automatically tilt the clubface
forward and so decrease its loft. Keep your head still and take a
three-quarter backswing and a three-quarter follow-through; don't
try and power this shot in an effort to beat the wind, simply keep
your swing smooth and controlled. Hit down into the ball more
abruptly than you would on a normal shot and make sure your
hands are leading the clubhead. Still keep the hands leading at
impact and aim to hit the ball as square as possible.

CROSSWIND (RIGHT TO LEFT)

When the wind blows from right to left across the fairway, length
is not so much affected as your aim. Balance is still important so
place your feet slightly wider apart and aim down the right-hand
side of the fairway. Take a normal easy swing and hit the ball with
authority. At first the wind will have little effect on the ball,
but as it nears the end of its flight and loses its forward power,
it will drift with the wind back into the centre of the fairway. These
conditions are, of course, perfect for the habitual slicer. He simply
aims straight for the target and lets the wind straighten out his
slice. Unfortunately it is not such a happy time for the golfer who
has a tendency to hook everything. He has two choices, he can aim
right and eliminate any wrist roll at the moment of impact or
simply line up his shot, making allowances for the amount of hook
and wind drift he can expect.

CROSSWIND (LEFT TO RIGHT)

A left to right wind blowing across the fairway can make things
difficult for every class of golfer. My advice is to 'hood' the face
of the club slightly, by that I mean turn the toe of the club towards
the target at address. Take your normal stance and grip and aim
down the left-hand side of the fairway. Here again, take an easy
swing and hit the ball with authority. Our friend, the slicer, can
find himself in double figures on these holes, unless he takes great

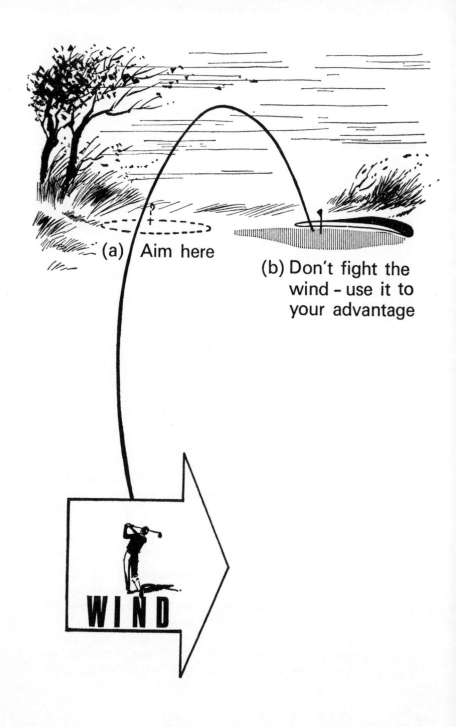

(a) Aim here

(b) Don't fight the
wind – use it to
your advantage

WIND

care to calculate the amount of slice and wind drift he can expect. Now the golfer who tends to hook everything can aim the ball straight at the target and let the wind straighten out his hook.

DOWN WIND

Tee the ball a little higher and swing easily. With a wind at your back you can expect extra run on all shots so allow for it, don't let your ball run into trouble. You can also expect not only extra distance but extra accuracy as well. A good strong following wind will help straighten out a slice or a hook; whereas a similar shot of this nature would have found the rough on a normal day, it will now land safely on the fairway.

It is a mistake to step onto the tee in these conditions, determined to slam the ball a couple of miles down the fairway. This great temptation to try and hit the ball extra hard must be resisted. It upsets your rhythm and timing—you usually end up hitting the ball off centre, sending it hardly any distance at all. Concentrate on a smooth controlled swing and be satisfied to let the wind work for you—then you will be pleasantly surprised just how far your ball travels.

TAKE A TIP . . .

Many golfers toss a few blades of grass into the air to judge the strength and direction of the wind. This can often be very deceiving, for the wind near ground level is not necessarily the same as that high up where your ball will travel. Far better to check the topmost branches of a tree.

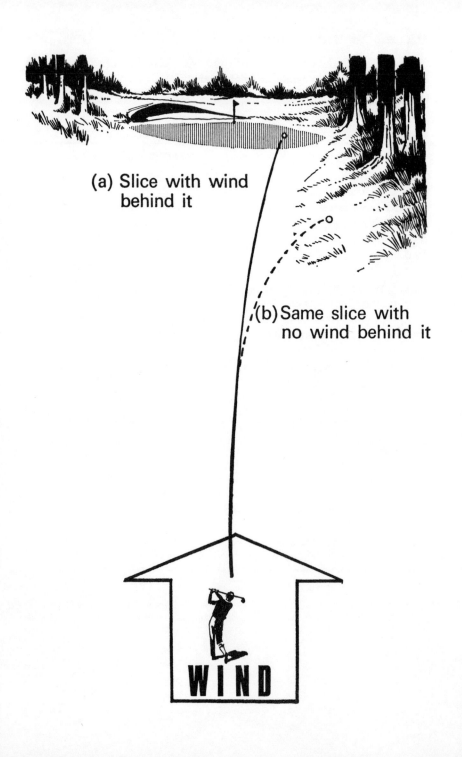

(a) Slice with wind behind it

(b) Same slice with no wind behind it

WIND

15

WET-WEATHER GOLF

Wet weather provides the ninety shooter with a water-tight alibi when he fluffs a shot—'My foot slipped' he'll say or 'My grip was wet'. Excuses such as these are always accepted, with a smile of course—for golf in wet weather makes shot-making twice as hard. The only way you will succeed is not to blame the weather but to beat it. Good Golf can be played in the rain if you are prepared to dress sensibly and play sensibly.

DRESS

(A) Check those spikes in your shoes. If they are well worn put new ones in. The careless golfers who play with well worn spikes are doomed from the start. As soon as your feet slip, your balance is destroyed and with it your rhythm and timing. Should you still be lucky enough to hit the ball you will have to be doubly lucky to hit the fairway—remember a firm footing is the first essential in good golf. While we are on the subject of shoes, don't wear ones that let in water or you will soon find that cold wet feet do not help your golf, or for that matter your temper.

(B) Put on a cap when it rains—wet hair has a nasty habit of dripping water down the back of your neck. This not only causes discomfort, it plays havoc with your concentration.

(C) Put on a pair of waterproof trousers and a jacket as soon as it starts raining—don't delay—it is a mistake to gamble on the rain easing off. If it doesn't you will have to put your waterproofs on over wet clothes—or leave them off altogether—either way your golf is ruined. Also make sure your jacket is on the big side, you must have plenty of room or you will not have the freedom to swing the club freely.

(D) Always carry two extra gloves so you will be able to change when they get too wet. I have found that ordinary cotton gloves give a much better grip than leather ones.

(E) Carry at least two small hand towels. These will be helpful in keeping your grips dry and also for wiping your hands on.

(F) If your golf bag has no hood—get one. It is essential to cover your clubs as soon as it rains, once your grips get wet there is nothing you can do about it.

A good umbrella will now eliminate any possible chance of you getting wet. Having taken these precautions you can forget the rain and concentrate on the problems of playing on a wet course.

PLAYING ON A SOAKED FAIRWAY

Don't overswing—a three-quarter backswing and three-quarter follow-through is all that is required in these conditions—you must *swing easy* and *hit hard*.

One thing you must avoid is hitting behind the ball. If your clubhead digs in too far on soft wet turf it will force you to quit on the shot and the ball will fall well short of its target. Then again, take a small divot before you hit the ball and the chances are you will get a 'flier' and possibly turn a six iron into a five or even a four. This is because the water from the grass fills the grooves on the clubface and makes it impossible for it to grip the ball at impact. A ball struck in this manner flies off with considerable top spin and doesn't bite properly when it lands. So on wet turf it is necessary to pick the ball off cleanly. To do this, at address, position the ball well forward off your left foot. This will enable you to hit the ball cleanly on the upswing. Don't take chances with these shots, aim for the biggest part of the green, and keep well clear of bunkers.

PUTTING ON WET GREENS

On wet greens the ball travels through the soft wet grass, which means sidehill putts break less than they would on dry greens. Wet greens are also slower than dry ones so you can afford to be

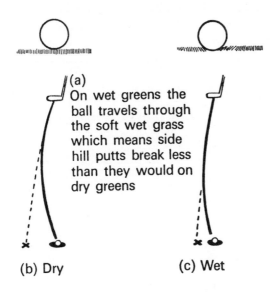

(a)
On wet greens the ball travels through the soft wet grass which means side hill putts break less than they would on dry greens

(b) Dry   (c) Wet

bold and strike the ball firmly for the back of the cup. There is very little fear of the ball rolling far past if you are a little off line.

A word of warning—never be foolish enough to play golf in a thunderstorm. Lightning usually strikes in that deadly lull before the rain, make sure you are back in the clubhouse before the first flash. Golfers are especially susceptible to lightning because golf is played in a large open space and the conditions are ideal for lightning attacks. There will be times when you find it impossible to reach the clubhouse before the thunderstorm strikes, in that case avoid the following:

E.G.—G

(1) A tall exposed tree
(2) Metal fences of any description
(3) High ground
(4) Any small shelter

If the storm is particularly savage don't be too proud—jump into a deep depression—even it it's only a bunker.

I cannot overstress how important it is to leave the course when lightning is about. Each year the number of golfers killed on golf courses is mounting. Agreed, more golfers are taking up the game each year, but then, just as many are reckless and take unnecessary chances—chances which endanger their lives.

TAKE A TIP . . .

Buy a pair of cotton gloves, they are excellent for giving a secure grip in wet weather.

16

GETTING OUT OF TROUBLE

To see your drive miss the fairway and head towards some trees is just about the most disheartening sight on a golf course. You have time, too much time, in fact, to curse the shot as you walk towards the disaster area. You wonder if it is lost or poked away in some impossible position. Walter Hagen and Arnold Palmer built up their reputations with recovery shots from these card-wrecking situations. But for my money the greatest recovery artist of all time was Jimmy Bruen. Bruen had enormously strong arms and hands which enabled him to make light of the 'heaviest rough'. Half-buried, grass covered balls which today's golfer wouldn't attempt to play, Bruen would knock out with tremendous power. On many occasions the ball would scream out leaving him standing there holding just a grip. In fact, 'club buster' Bruen used to break an iron in almost every round he played.

Unfortunately there are very few Palmers, Hagens or Bruens in golf, so when you find your ball in the deep rough, trapped behind trees, or in a disastrous lie, resist the temptation to try the impossible. The good golfer knows when to draw the line between being *aggressive* and being *foolish*. At all times keep calm, consider the risks and the consequences of failure. Discipline yourself not to

think of playing two shots in one. It is madness to try and escape
your predicament and recover lost ground all with one shot. If the
odds are against you don't gamble, even it if means you have to
chip out onto the fairway away from the green. I have seen club
golfers blaze away at impossible shots which no professional
would even attempt. Such foolhardiness means they throw away
three or four strokes before they finally hack the ball out onto the
fairway.

Having decided to play a safety shot, don't be lulled into thinking it is a simple shot—or the chances are you will fail with this
just as easily. A four wood can be used to great effect in the rough,
provided, of course, you are satisfied you have a reasonable lie.
You can expect to hit the ball a very long way with this club because
it doesn't get strangled by the grass like an iron does. The wooden
head spreads the grass, an iron blade tears through it, losing
valuable clubhead speed in the process. Another reason why the
four wood is so effective in the rough is because it has so much loft
on the clubface. The only way out of long grass is through the air
and this club is designed to throw the ball up quickly. *For this
reason never use a long iron out of long rough.*

When the ball is lying well down in the grass, use a short iron
club if need be, the wedge. Break your wrists quickly in the
backswing, this will prevent the grass from catching round the
clubhead. Hit down sharply with plenty of wrist action and don't
quit on the shot.

The ball below your feet on a side slope is a tricky enough shot
as it is. To have to play it in the rough can shatter the confidence
of the most hardened golfer. Firstly don't be too ambitious as far
as distance is concerned, getting the ball out is your main problem.
Take your pitching wedge but don't grip too far down the shaft, we
need the club length to get down to the ball. Having established a
firm footing, keep your weight on your heels and bend from the
knees, emphasising the 'sitting' position. Break your wrists quickly
as you take the club back and avoid overswinging. A half shot is all
we need here. Hit down sharply and don't try to scoop the ball
up. Keep the clubhead going through low at impact and well into
the follow-through (see illustration), stay down with this shot until
the ball is safely up and away. This is a swing with the arms and
hands only, keep the leg work down to a minimum.

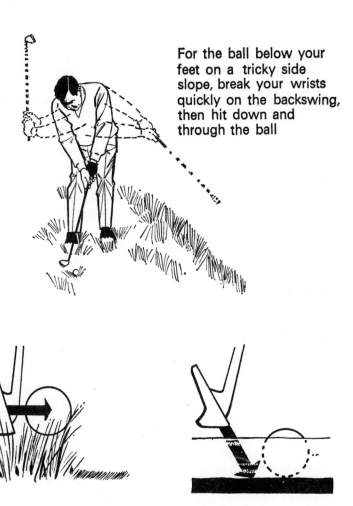

For the ball below your
feet on a tricky side
slope, break your wrists
quickly on the backswing,
then hit down and
through the ball

For the ball perched up
two or three inches in
high rough, don't ground
the club, place it directly
behind the ball

In shallow water, when
your ball isn't entirely
submerged, take your
pitching wedge, open
the blade and play it
like a bunker shot

When your ball has come to rest so near to a tree that there is insufficient room for a full backswing, it doesn't mean you have to settle for a half-hearted stab at the ball. With a few adjustments and a little thought you may be able to let go with big a swing yet. In order to gain as much room for your backswing as possible, address the ball off your right toe. Should this little manœuvre not gain enough extra space select your shortest club and grip well down the shaft. Now try a practice swing, if your clubhead doesn't brush the tree all is well. You must appreciate that when you address the ball off your right toe, your hands will be well in front of the clubhead, automatically closing the clubface. This could result in you smothering the shot, to correct this, open the clubface.

Keeping your weight on your left side, break your wrists as soon as you start the backswing. Don't get greedy. An overswing will only succeed in upsetting your balance. Now swing down sharply and hit with authority. You will be surprised at the distance which can be achieved from this very cramped but useful swing.

When you find your ball in a divot hole resist the temptation to scoop it out. At address, position the ball in the middle of your stance with your hands well in front of the ball. Keep your weight favouring your left side throughout the swing. With your hands leading the clubhead, hit down on the ball. You can expect a low-flying shot with plenty of roll.

A ball perched up two or three inches off the ground in high rough is not such a simple shot as it appears at first glance. I, myself, have been guilty of scything under the ball and leaving it just a little lower, but still in the same place. In these circumstances don't ground the club, place it directly behind the ball. Play the shot this way and you will pick the ball off cleanly.

When your ball lands in a water hazard, I'm afraid there is little you can do. Water bends light rays at odd angles, giving a false picture of the ball's position. Then again, water is difficult to compress, so take my advice and drop out and accept the penalty. Of course, if it is in shallow water and the ball isn't entirely submerged, you can have a go—take your pitching wedge, open the blade and play it like a bunker shot. *Don't expect to get a lot of distance, but do expect to get wet!*

TAKE A TIP . . .

The only way to perfect any shot in golf is to practise it. This also applies to recovery shots in the rough, sand traps and other such hazards. So find similar situations on your course to practise in.

17

SPECIAL SHOTS FOR SPECIAL OCCASIONS

Golf courses have been designed to penalise bad shots. Sometimes the penalty is light and the golfer is left with a straightforward shot from the rough. But on other occasions he may not be so fortunate, a tree, fence or bush can put him in an out-of-the-ordinary position. In these cases don't panic, the answer is to play an out-of-the-ordinary shot. Until the day comes when somebody invents a club with a rubber shaft which will bend round these obstacles, you will have to rely on an unorthodox shot to get at the ball. An unorthodox swing can and will perform the job of a normal swing, although, of course, to a slightly lesser degree.

Problem: Ball up against high rushes preventing normal swing.

When an obstruction prevents you from taking a normal swing at the ball reverse your stance and use a left-hander's swing. Don't be too ambitious, your muscles are not trained for a swing from the opposite side. Concentrate on a slower, shorter and more deliberate swing. Grip well down the shaft, left hand below right. On these occasions turn the blade of the club upside down (see illustration). Keep your right arm straight on the backswing, just as you would keep your left arm straight in a normal swing. There

will be a natural tendency to bend the right arm, don't—or you will top the shot. Keep your eye on the ball and concentrate on meeting it squarely with the clubhead. Use a four or five iron if you want to keep the ball low, an eight or nine if you require loft. This is an excellent shot for getting out of trouble and one you should never be afraid to attempt.

Problem: Ball on top lip of steep banked bunker.

This is the shot the average club golfer tries to pick off with a flat self-invented swing. Invariably he shanks the shot, shooting the ball off at right angles. Although on occasions I have seen golfers actually knock the ball behind them back into the bunker. The smart way to play this shot is to take your putter, stand on top of the banking and play a left-handed shot. You can achieve quite a considerable distance when hitting the ball this way.

Problem: Ball at front of bunker on steep uphill lie.

The high-handicapped golfer ties himself into all sorts of knots

trying to play this shot. He places his left foot on top of the bank and digs his right foot into the side banking. Unable to place extra weight on his left foot to keep from swaying backwards he wobbles badly on the backswing, panics, and attempts to chop down on the ball. Unless luck is on his side he fails with the stroke and has to start all over again. The correct way to play this trouble shot is simplicity itself. By kneeling with your left leg on top of the banking you will be able to shift extra weight onto your left side. With your balance problem solved, grip well down the shaft and concentrate on a slower, shorter swing. Don't quit on the shot, let the clubhead travel through into the banking. Play it this way and you will be surprised how easy this trouble shot really is.

Problem: Ball up against big tree which prevents normal swing.

Many club golfers don't stop to think in a situation like this. They knock the ball away with a back-handed shot and start again. Take my advice, turn your back on the problem and it's solved. By

turning your back to the target you can address the ball one-handed. For tighter control of the shot, grip well down the shaft with your right hand. Keep your hand in *front* of the ball as you swing slowly back and then down. It is possible to hit the ball some fifty to sixty yards with ease this way.

Problem: Ball in rough near top of slope at back of green.

Many club golfers automatically try to chip the ball down onto the green. Sometimes they succeed, but just as often they don't. So why take chances when there is a much simpler way to play such an exacting shot? The problem here can be easily overcome if you use your putter. Don't baby the putt, strike it with authority, but take care that you hit the top half of the ball only. This way the top

Use your putter when you find your ball in the rough at the top of a slope, at the back of a green. Aim to strike the top half of the ball only

of the ball moves first towards the hole and not the bottom. It will now run quite easily through the rough and down the slope. If you have timed the shot correctly it will finish up close to the flag and on occasions there will the ones that drop.

TAKE A TIP . . .

When you find your ball in trouble, always take the easiest route out. You are not looking for an out-of-this-world shot, you are looking for an out-of-the-rough shot. Your one object is to get the ball back in play.

18

COMMON FAULTS

The hardest shot to hit in golf is the straight one. The most infuriating is the slice, the most damaging is the hook, the most demoralising is the shank and the most embarrassing is the topped one. Yet everybody who takes up this wonderful game of golf will at one time or another hit all these shots. The only difference between the beginner and the top professional is that the pro makes fewer mistakes. Always remember it is not the golfer who makes the most birdies who wins the tournament—it's the one who makes the fewest mistakes.

For the beginner to always try and solve these problems unaided can mean months of frustration where the misses begin to outnumber the hits. The cure for his golfing ills can easily be found by seeking the advice of a club professional who is trained to spot such things quickly. From my own teaching experience I have found that a great many faults which beset the weekender can be traced directly to a simple fundamental in the swing which has been overlooked.

THE SLICE

The most common single fault among golfers is slicing. Some allow

for the slice and in many cases play quite a reasonable game with
it. Others finally lose heart and give up playing golf altogether.
Why the slice causes so many headaches defeats me, for this is one
fault that can be easily cured. The reason for a slice is an out-to-in
swing with the clubface open to the line of flight at the moment of
impact. This produces a clockwise spin which will make the ball
curve to the right during flight. If you suffer from a slice the
first place to check is your grip. Stand before a full-length mirror

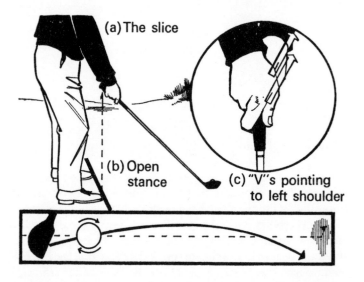

(a) The slice

(b) Open
stance

(c) "V"'s pointing
to left shoulder

and have a good look at the 'V's formed by the thumb and fore-
fingers of your hands. If the 'V's point towards your left shoulder
or chin then you are gripping the club incorrectly. If you ever hope
to hit the ball straight again you must alter this damaging grip.
Hold the club with your left hand so you can see two knuckles.
Now grip with your right hand so that the 'V' formed by the thumb
and forefinger points between your right cheek and shoulder.

    Another cause for slicing is having an open stance. If your left
foot is behind your right at address, there is a tendency to take the
club back outside the line in the backswing and return it along an
outside-in path on the downswing. This means the clubhead will
cut across the ball and produces a clockwise-slice spin. To rectify
this take a square stance, this means an imaginary line drawn across

your feet is aimed directly at the flag. From this stance you will find it easy to take the club back square to the target line. Now see to it that you have a full shoulder turn, get your left shoulder under and not round the chin. On the downswing turn your hips towards the hole and make sure your right shoulder is starting *down* and not *around*.

Then, again, lots of weekend golfers try to hit the ball too late and the hands move ahead of the ball in the hitting area. In these cases the clubhead has insufficient time to catch up with them at impact. This results in the clubface still being open when it strikes the ball. Leave it to the professionals who are playing golf every day and have tremendously strong hands to produce this late hit. I strongly advise you to make a point of accelerating the clubhead the moment the hands pass the hips in the downswing. This will give the hands sufficient time to square up the clubface at impact. It also serves a double purpose, for it helps shift your weight onto your left foot.

THE HOOK

This is when your ball generally starts out towards the target, then swerves in flight finishing far to the left. Basically a hook results from an in-to-out swing with the clubface turned to the left—or

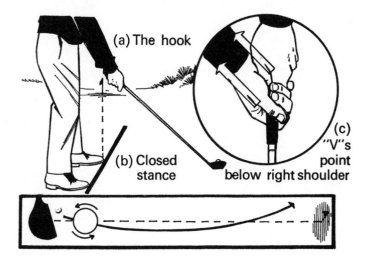

(a) The hook

(c) "V"s point below right shoulder

(b) Closed stance

closed—at impact. When this happens, the imparting counter-clockwise spin produces a violent hooking action. Once again the first place to check for such a fault is the grip. Look at your right hand, it may have moved too far under the shaft with the result that the 'V' formed by the thumb and forefinger of that hand is pointing well outside your right shoulder. At address make sure that you can only see two knuckles on your left hand and that the 'V's of both hands point to a position between your right shoulder and chin.

Now check your stance; it could be that you are using a closed one. This means your left foot is in front of your right. With this stance the player takes his club back too much inside the target line and returns the club to the ball with in-to-out action increasing his hooking problem. At address make sure your feet, hips and shoulders face directly at the target. If you cannot do this with your eyes alone, take a club and lay it in line with your feet. If the club points straight at the target then you have the required square stance.

TOPPING

There is nothing more infuriating than topping a golf ball and seeing an intended long hit finish up just a few yards ahead of you. A topped shot is simply the clubhead contacting the ball above

The golfer who crouches too much at add-ress, tends to straighten on the backswing, resulting in a topped shot

centre. The most common cause of this fault is when the golfer
tries, subconsciously, to scoop the ball up. In these cases the player
leans his weight to the right on the downswing, trying to put his
body under the ball, so to speak. This results in an upward lift of
the arms and hands which causes the clubhead to rise abruptly as
it contacts the ball. Do have faith in the club you have selected,
they all have sufficient built-in loft to put the golf ball in the air.
It does not require any scooping action by you to achieve this object.

Then again, a golfer who tends to top his shots reasons wrongly
that he must get closer to the ball, so he bends his knees more.
This results in him straightening them on the backswing and the
inevitable happens—the clubhead catches the ball above centre.
Don't overflex your knees at address, this will eliminate the tendency to straighten up on the backswing, and helps you to recap-
ture your address position at impact.

A bent left arm at impact can also cause a topped shot. Remember the left arm acts as the radius of the swing and it's the way we
measure ourselves from the ball. So concentrate on keeping the
left arm straight at impact, and follow through keeping the clubhead
close to the ground. *This way you will ensure that your swing radius
remains constant throughout the swing.*

You could well be topping your shots because your right

A high right   shoulder and a
bent left arm at impact can also
result in a topped shot

shoulder is too high at impact. If your right shoulder is still up in the hitting area so too is the clubhead. Here again the ball will be sent racing along the ground. The cure is simple, get your right shoulder to swing under your chin in the hitting area.

SHANKING

Any golfer who has a tendency to shank has my sympathy. This shot can and will destroy a golfer's confidence completely. The shot that the shank produces is a horror, it shoots that ball off at almost right angles to the target. The reason for this is that the golf ball is being struck with the neck of the club instead of the clubface. The weekender's first reaction to a bad shank is to stand further away from the ball for his next shot. Then, with extra care, he swings and tries again. Now he is in trouble, for not only has he shanked it, he's probably put it in the rough. By standing further away from the ball he increased his problem—because his swing became even flatter. To cure a shank you must stand nearer to the ball and accentuate the tilting and turning of the shoulders. By doing this you form a more upright swing—which enables the clubface to meet the ball squarely at impact.

Then again, watch that the distance between your right foot and the ball is not too little. If your right foot is too near this brings the right shoulder over, rolls the clubface at impact and a shut-face shank results, the ball being jammed out of the heel and socket of the club.

TAKE A TIP . . .

I think it was Harry Vardon who said 'I love to play against a man with a straight left arm'. Sound thinking, for too many golfers interpret 'straight' as 'stiff'. Golf is not a stiff game, some lines do go straight but never stiff. Stiffness always leads to lack of rhythm and when that goes so does your swing.

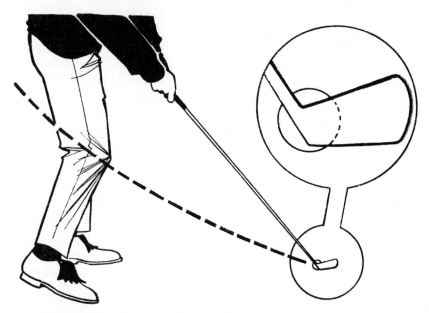

(a) By standing too far away from the ball, your swing becomes too flat and the chances are you will shank the ball

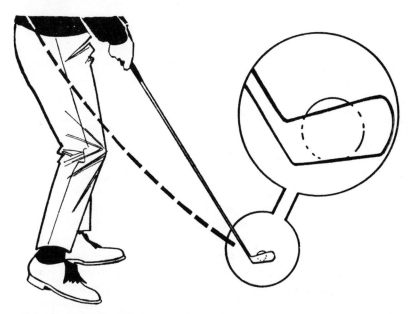

(b) To cure a shank, stand nearer to the ball. By doing this you form a more upright swing which enables the clubface to meet the ball squarely

19

THE RIGHT SWING FOR YOUR BUILD

Golf is a game which is definitely more difficult for those of extremes. The very tall golfer, the very short golfer and the very round golfer have their own different swing problems.

The very tall golfer has to contend with a big swing radius—left shoulder to clubhead—which is naturally too wide for the short game. For the very short golfer, he has the problems in reverse. His shorter radius—left shoulder to clubhead—has too narrow a swing arc for his wooden shots.

This is not to say these golfers never become good players. Little men like Gene Sarazen and Gary Player have shown it can be done. So have tall golfers such as Cary Middlecoff and George Archer. In general a tall golfer, to avoid bending too much at the waist, stands nearer to the ball and therefore swings more upright. The shorter golfer, to avoid holding his clubs at chest height, naturally stands farther away and has a flatter swing.

Another vital measurement is that around the middle. Heavyweights Jack Nicklaus and Bobby Locke have proved that the extra poundage does not in any way restrict freedom of play. But then they have learned to use their extra poundage to advantage. For the heavyweight golfer to do this he must guard against using an

The short golfer stands farther away from the ball and has a flatter swing than the tall golfer who, to avoid bending too much, stands nearer to the ball and swings more upright

open stance—right foot in front of left, for it increases the difficulty of executing a full turn on the backswing. The heavyweight should also bend slightly more from the waist than normal. This will encourage a definite tilting of the shoulders and avoid too flat a swing, the most common fault among the 'heavies'. Take the club back slowly and smoothly. You need time to shift your extra poundage. Start the downswing with your left hip, this moves your middle out of the way and makes room for your hands and arms to swing through the hitting area. Don't 'quit' on the shot, and take your arms through to a nice high finish.

It is sometimes helpful to model your swing on a golfer who resembles closely your own physical attributes. It would be ridiculous, and also very wrong, for a short man of slight stature to try and emulate Jack Nicklaus' very powerful upright swing.

Heavyweights should bend slightly more from the waist than normal to encourage a definite tilting of the shoulders during the swing

Doug Sanders has said he has the perfect 'weekend golfer's swing' and this, in some ways, is true. I don't go along with those who criticise Sanders' action because they feel it is too gimmicky. His short three-quarter backswing, so compact and beautifully controlled, it hardly, if ever, gets him into trouble. I strongly advise golfers, who are getting on in years and have possibly thickened up round the middle, to adopt a three-quarter backswing. Why struggle to do a big sweeping swing which can sometimes prove too much even for those with young supple bodies? Agreed, in Sanders' case he is young enough not to have to settle for such a short swing, but would a long one suit him better? I don't think so, he gets nearly as much distance with his short swing as he would with a longer one. For the few yards he loses in length, he gains in direction.

Doug, of course, generates a lot of his power from his tremendous hand action. When the body plays a minor role in the swing the hands must predominate. In fact Sanders uses his hands to such an extent he has to tape together the first two fingers of his right hand, otherwise he splits the skin in between as he whips his hands through at impact. I honestly believe the average week-ender overswings in an effort to gain extra yardage. In most cases they fail because this overswinging leads them into hitting with the shoulders. Three-quarter to horizontal is as far as the club should travel in the backswing. *In fact there is not one world-class golfer playing today whose backswing goes much below the horizontal.*

It is a pity that more manufacturers do not supply tailor-made clubs for the extra tall or short golfers as part of their normal service. Admittedly all the manufacturers will make up a tailor-made set, but for this extra special service you sometimes have to pay more. Also you must be prepared to be patient, for this can be rather a lengthy process. But in every case, it is one well worth waiting for. I know, from my own experience, how essential it is that these players be catered for individually—they must have tailor-made clubs, if they are ever to master the swing problems that their uncommon heights present.

Of course, I am talking now of the 6 ft. 4 in. seventeen stone man and 5 ft. 3 in. seven stone man. Unfortunately at the moment golf is geared for Mr. Average, which means that these golfers have to try and master their difficult swing arcs with inadequate clubs.

TAKE A TIP . . .

The best lady golfers I have seen in our country, i.e. Jean Donald, Jessie Valentine and Angela Bonallack, all used clubs that felt super to me. So don't be ashamed of using lightweight clubs, they can, and will, knock shots of your game.

20

THE CORRECT WAY TO PRACTISE

All the world's top golfers will tell you after they have played a round of golf that only a few of the shots have been struck perfectly the remainder were hit slightly off the centre of the clubface. (Even so the ball came off straight enough and in many cases earned applause from the packed galleries.) This means the golfer's search for perfection must go on, and the only place he will find it is out there on the practice ground.

When you are out on the practice ground always remember you are out there to build up your swing rhythm, you cannot simulate actual playing conditions or pressures there. I feel twenty minutes with twenty balls and maximum concentration is worth at least two hours of thoughtless slogging with 2,000. Always select a suitable target to aim at, it could be a bush, a bunker, a tree, anything. This will cut out the temptation to try and out-hit each successive shot. The purpose of practising is to repeatedly hit that ball straight and at a consistent length. Don't practise from bad lies unless you are trying to play these particular shots; you must hit the ball off level ground if you hope to groove a repeating swing. That's all golf is, a repeating swing, whether it be a pretty one like Sam Snead's or rather an ugly one like Jack Nicklaus', once it repeats, you can make it work for you.

To practise with old misshapen golf balls is wrong, save these for bunker practice. Every dimple is there for a purpose and when a ball gets damaged, it rarely flies true and this can mislead you into thinking you are not striking it correctly. Also always take the trouble to clean your practice balls before use, one seems to concentrate more on a clean ball than a dirty cut one. I have actually seen golfers who have spent five minutes hitting dirty golf balls, trudge off and spend twice as long trying to find them. So make a point of keeping them clean. It makes finding them so much easier and quicker. The purpose of a practice session is to spend time hitting balls, not looking for them.

Make your practice interesting or you will soon become bored and careless and this only leads to harm. Try and introduce a competitive flavour into these sessions. Set yourself targets. For example, if you are ironing out your chipping problems it is sometimes a good idea to place a golf ball on the ground a few yards in front of you. Now try to get twelve chip shots to stop inside an imaginary three-foot circle round the ball.

Practise hitting from the rough, this is a marvellous all-round conditioner. The grass will offer resistance to your clubhead, forcing you to hit down and through the ball. This is a very helpful exercise for those golfers who have a habit of quitting on the shot. Also forcing the club through the grass in this manner helps strengthen your golf muscles. A word of caution—brute strength is not called for here, so don't swing wildly. Use a controlled swing and concentrate on hitting the ball first and getting it up and away.

Never approach the practice ground without a purpose or a problem to be solved. If your problem is a serious one, like a bad slice or a chronic shank, seek professional guidance first, then you will be able to go out and practise the right things. Unfortunately many thoughtless golfers only practise their faults.

It is a pity that some clubs haven't a practice ground, which can mean club members have to practise hitting into a net. This sort of practice can be deceiving, for what looks a perfectly good shot could well move off line later in flight. The purpose of a net is to stop the ball, it does not allow the golfer to see the result of his shot. But some good is derived from net practice, even if it's only keeping the golfer's muscles nicely tuned up.

THE PRACTICE GREEN

It is very difficult to practise putting because the putts you will actually have to face out there on the course will hardly represent those on the practice green. The various slopes and borrows which make every green so different, can only be tackled in an actual round. Although the practice green is ideal for practising both short and long putts. One way of doing this is to stand on the edge of the putting green with twelve balls. Now try to hit them up to the hole inside an imaginary three-foot circle. You'll be surprised how many you will actually drop—this, of course, will do wonders for your confidence. If you're bad on the three-foot putts, practise from twelve to eighteen inches, get used to the ball going *into the hole*.

A good way to practise leaving those long putts close to the hole is to stand on the edge of the green with twelve balls. Now try to hit them up to the hole inside an imaginary three foot circle. You will be surprised how many will actually drop

For some odd reasons if you practise hard in the British Isles you become a pot hunter in a lot of peoples' eyes, which, of course, is ridiculous. Golf is like life, you only get out of it what you put into it. In professional golf this sort of attitude just does not exist. In fact there is a lot of camaraderie amongst golfers especially on the practice ground. Before a tournament you might be having trouble with your driving. So you walk up to another golfer, possibly a friend of yours, and tell him the problem. In every case he will be only too willing to take time off and try to put things right for you. Now it's quite possible you may go out, beat him and win the tournament in the process. Now could you imagine two boxers, before a big fight, having a similar talk? Perhaps one asking the other to straighten out the trouble he is having with his right hook? Of course not. It's things like this which make golf the truly wonderful game it is.

TAKE A TIP . . .

If you keep your head still, look at the ball and swing at it with any degree of rhythm, you must be, at worst, *twelve handicap*.

21

THE MENTAL APPROACH

A golfer walks alone—I often wish I had been in a sport in which I was one of a team. Then when things went wrong the blame was not mine to shoulder alone. Imagine you are a racing car driver, how wonderful to be able to say 'I would have won but the carburettor went' or 'the engine packed up'. Then there's the goalkeeper, beaten by a seemingly simple shot—'I never saw it' he'll say 'my team mates unsighted me'. The only reason I lose a tournament is because I knock a ball out of bounds or I miss a couple of silly two-foot putts. I can't blame it on my clubs, they didn't break in half, nor did the ball explode, there's no excuses. Nothing to blame, but myself.

Panic in golf is purely the time factor, you get nervous at any game. The tennis player who walks onto the Centre Court at Wimbledon is nervous, but only until the player at the other end steps back and serves, and then wham! The ball comes over the net, the time factor is over, there's no more nervous waiting, you're in there playing. Football, cricket, rugby, they're all the same—the ball is hammered at you and you react instinctively. There is less time to think and therefore the great mental pressures in these sports would seem to be less. Whereas in golf you go to

the first tee, possibly leading the tournament and tee up. You try
hard to control your nerves as you take aim, swing and hit that
ball. You watch it fly away—it's not too straight and it lands 290
yards away on the left of the fairway. Now you've got a four-
minute walk to that ball, alone with your thoughts. The mental
pressures mount again as you plan your next shot—you're none
too happy with your position. You think as you walk to the ball—
but are interrupted by the gallery passing their remarks. You try
not to listen, but somehow they filter into your mind. 'I can't see
him winning this tournament,' says one, another 'What an idiot,
hitting it there, you'd think he would have had enough sense to
put it nearer to the middle of the fairway!' You feel an impulse to
stop and say 'Thank you very much for the compliments!' But
of course you don't, you simply stride off, your eyes fixed on the
ball ahead. Their remarks have done nothing to bolster your
confidence, yet somehow you manage to hit the ball on the green.
The clapping tells you it's landed near the flag—but it dies sudden-
ly; this is an indication that the putt will still be a long one.
You've got two selves talking to each other in your head as you
stand over the putt. One of them is saying 'I can't hole this, it's
downhill, it's fast and it's bumpy—and if I hit it too hard. . . .'
And then the other voice interrupts and says 'Come on, don't be
so bloody silly, of course you can do it, go on—bang it in!' The
battle rages and whichever one of these two voices wins the
argument determines the fate of the putt. I'm sure Arnold Palmer
never suffers from this, he has just one voice saying 'You can do it,
Arnie, go on, boy! Go for the green.' He could be up to his chin
in high rough and still that little voice urges him on. 'Go on,
Arnie, you can bang this one on!' and nine times out of ten he does.
The one word Arnold's little voice will never utter is 'can't'.

Gary Player is the same, but he labels it 'Positive Thinking'.
Gary will never let himself think he can possibly fluff a shot, he
keeps saying to himself 'I can do it—I can do it—I can do it'. It's a
sort of self-hypnosis. Personally I have never gone in for this,
although there's times I wish I could. I mean there's nothing I'd
like more than to be able to say to myself 'Eat a jam sandwich
before you go out and you'll sink every putt!' This is one of the
reasons why Dai Rees has been such a good player over the years.
He's absolutely convinced he has never hit a bad shot. It's never

been Dai's fault when a ball ends up in the rough, somebody used a camera, moved in the gallery, spoke to him, there was mud on the ball, a bad lie, foot slipped, studs are gone—the list is endless. But this is good for Dai and in a way we're all like this. The moment you start blaming yourself and not the elements, that's when the big doubts come in, the problems start—you've had it. Of course, nobody else accepts these excuses—you only have to read the papers after the tournament to prove this. Failure is yours alone—but then, so are your successes.

I've asked every world-class golfer if he actually enjoyed playing tournament golf, if he enjoyed going out to compete when in a winning position. Only three players admitted to getting some sort of enjoyment out of situations like this. Nagle, Palmer and Rees. These three basically just live to play golf. Their idea of a day off would not be complete unless it included a round of golf with a friend. They are simply in love with the game. Everything about big-time golf appeals to them; they are stimulated by the gallery, big crowds help spur them on. Whereas some top-class golfers find their concentration is affected by the pressure a big crowd atmosphere creates. This is the reason why they never produce their best scores when they need them most.

Possibly this is why Jack Nicklaus is such a great tournament player. Absolutely nothing destroys his concentration. His every movement is thoughtful, deliberate and unhurried. He plays as though he's the only man on the course. He will never start his backswing until he is ready, time is not important, but the shot is. I've seen Jack hit a few bad shots, but never seen him hit a careless one. For me he's just about the best mentally-equipped golfer in the game today.

I sometimes create unnecessary fears for myself. For instance, I have always had a mental fear of topping a shot completely. I never ever have, so why should I have this feeling? I can't explain, but I do. It's more often than not when I take a wooden club on the fairway. Hence the importance of hitting through the ball with your weight on your left leg. Ben Hogan is the best I have ever seen for getting his weight onto the left leg at impact, which is why he is one of the finest strikers the game has ever known.

Some golfers combat this mental problem with superstitions. Harry Weetman for instance, when he won his match play championships, wore the same clothes every day—same trousers, same pullover, same everything. Casper and Player must always have a new golf glove in every round they play. Player also uses up to eighteen golf balls in a round, he will not use a ball if it contains even the slightest graze, speck or blemish. Kel Nagle once got very attached to a putter—unfortunately for Kel the grip was wearing out. In fact, it was breaking up into tiny pieces and these were held together by Sellotape. Eventually he couldn't use it any longer, so he took all the little bits to the factory, to be carefully weighed. Kel had to be sure that the new grip would keep the weight and balance of his favourite putter exactly the same. Peter Thomson has no superstitions whatsoever. He'll unwrap a new set of woods and go straight out and play in a tournament with them. I know of nobody else who will dare to do this, the majority of golfers will have to play three or four weeks with the clubs to get the feel of them.

I agree with Thomson. I feel it is much better if you can get by without any superstitions at all. I myself, have been guilty of not changing a slightly-damaged ball during a round when I have been doing remarkably well with it, even though it is beginning to wobble about in flight. But the worse it gets the more you are looking to drop a shot, so you can have an excuse to change it. This is bad and it's a trap which I make sure I do not fall into now. Even so, after I have had a particularly bad hole, I always pull out a ball with a number two or a number one on it and usually things go right again. I never play with a five or six in fact, anything over four. There's not many professionals I know that will play with a ball with a number higher than four. We all associate five, six, or seven with the score we may get on the hole, we don't mind taking a four on each hole because then we do a seventy-two. I can remember one tournament in the north of England when I took out a number five on a simple par three and finished up hacking my way out of a wood and scrambling a lucky five. I changed to a number three ball and promptly birdied the next hole which was a par four.

To me golf is a series of mental pictures which I slot into my mind when the occasion demands it. When standing on a tee facing a very tricky drive on a narrow fairway, I always slip in one of these pictures. For this particular problem I think 'What would

When standing on a tee, facing a very tricky drive on a narrow fairway, slip in a mental picture which calls for a simple straightforward tee-shot

you do if you were on the first tee at Parkstone?' I slip in my slide now—the scene changes—it's the first tee at Parkstone, so I say 'have you ever missed this fairway?—Never!' By now I can even visualise old Fred looking on, this one I can't miss, it couldn't be easier. So whack! . . . And I don't. I invariably send that ball 260 to 300 yards straight down the middle. For me this works ninety-nine times out of a hundred.

Try this one for yourself. If you have been practising chipping into the armchair at home and you find yourself facing a tricky chip with a bunker between you and the pin, slip in a mental picture. Now for you the scene changes—you're chipping into the old armchair again—'Have I ever missed the armchair?—*Never?*' Then just pop the ball up into the imaginary armchair and you'll find you are left with a simple little putt. If you can discipline your mind to see the flag as the old armchair, there is no reason at all why you should not play the shot correctly. But if you become obsessed with the bunker in front of you that's where your ball is going to finish up. For any tricky or awkward situation take out a mental slide and slip in a picture which calls for a simple straightforward shot. Now go ahead and play that shot. You'd be surprised how many times you succeed.

On short holes perspective makes the green appear a very small target from the tee. It is this perspective which plays tricks with your judgment and forces you, sometimes, into a tentative shot which invariably misses the green. A good way to rid yourself of this mental problem is to take a walk round the course one day and stand on the greens of the short holes and look back at the tees. You will be astounded at how big—*positively enormous*—the green looks now. Retain this mental picture when you are next on that tee and you'll never miss—what has been proved to your mind—such a big target.

Eighty per cent of golf is mental—it has to be. The golf swing itself takes, on average, four seconds. If you card a seventy you have only some four and a half minutes of actual play to show for it. Now a round of golf can take anything from three to four hours, so you are left with an unbearable amount of time for thinking, planning, worrying and hoping. As I've said many times, golf is played at a low physical pressure and always at a dangerously high mental one.

E.G.—I

If you have been practising chipping into an armchair
and you find yourself facing a tricky chip with a bunker
between you and the pin, slip in a mental picture of the
armchair and there is no reason at all why you should
not play the shot correctly

TAKE A TIP . . .

Don't be intimidated by the trouble spots on the course. Concentrate on the area on which you want your ball to land, not on the area you wish to avoid.

On short holes perspective makes the green appear very small which can lead you into playing a tentative shot. To correct this impression stand on the greens of the short holes and you will realise just how big they really are

22

CARE OF EQUIPMENT

I had just finished an exhibition match in the north of England and was about to leap into my car when I noticed two club members about to hit off on the first tee. 'Watch this,' shouted across the taller of the two as he teed up. So naturally I stopped and moved into a better position to see. With his feet wide apart, he took a careful look down the fairway. Satisfied, he commenced his backswing. Slowly, almost painfully, he took the club back. At shoulder height he stopped, waited a second or two, then, as if to catch the ball unawares, he swung violently down and hit it a tremendous blow. Quickly regaining his balance, he leant back on his club to watch his ball slice wildly towards a huge bunker. To this day I still don't know if that ball landed in the bunker, for the next thing I saw was a pair of legs fly in the air as the club he was leaning on gave way. He hit the ground a frightful wallop, then rolled over once and sat up. He was still holding his club which was now minus a head. *I heaved a sigh of relief. Thank goodness only one neck had been broken!*

The moral of the story is a simple one—don't lean on your club when waiting for your partner to play his shot, it places considerable strain on the neck of the club and will, in time, cause it to crack or, as in this case, break. So don't forget, club leaners are out this season. . . . *Club cleaners are in!*

Many golfers unnecessarily penalise themselves by playing with dirty clubs. An unclean grip makes your hold on the club insecure. Leather-type grips which have become hard and shiny will also slip in your hands. Rough them up by gently scraping them with the edge of a coin, then rub warm castor oil well into them and leave for a day or two. If by then they have not reverted to their original tackiness it is advisable to have new grips fitted. Rubber grips can also be revitalised by a good scrubbing with water, or by rubbing with sandpaper.

Check the heads of your wooden clubs occasionally. If they are slightly worn in places, revarnish or relacquer at once, otherwise moisture will creep in. A little furniture wax or polish will quickly smarten up the look of the heads and also give added protection. Make a point of always replacing the head covers after each shot with a wooden club. An unprotected wood can be easily dented by coming into contact with the irons. These little dents will, in time, lead to cracks and serious damage. Leaving them in the back of the car without head covers on, as some people do from Sunday to Sunday, is unforgiveable. Take a pride in your clubs, treat them with care and they will last you a lifetime.

The iron clubs take terrific punishment on sunbaked stony courses and the soles get badly dented and scarred. On rain-soaked courses they also suffer, getting badly mud-splattered. Keep a piece of cloth on your bag, a two-second wipe after each shot will keep your clubs in good trim. Nine out of ten high handicap golfers seem to think an occasional wipe on the grass is enough, this is a mistake, for it does not remove the sand and dirt which fill up the grooves on the clubface. If you let the scoring marks on your clubs get clogged their value is lost completely. An unclean clubface will not strike the ball crisply or impart the necessary backspin to hold the ball safely on the green. Use a wooden tee-peg to clean out the grooves, then wash the clubface thoroughly in soap and water. Dry with a piece of cloth and, if storing, it is advisable to coat them lightly with grease.

Check your spikes occasionally and if they are worn down replace them. The screw-in spikes which golfers favour today make this quite a simple job.

A golf glove is a sound investment but once it gets hard and worn and begins to feel uncomfortable, change it. Anything which can possibly interfere with your concentration is going to affect your game.

TAKE A TIP . . .

On cold winter days carry a little hand warmer in each pocket, they will keep your hands warm and also serve to warm two spare golf balls. Remember a 'cold' ball will travel fifteen to twenty yards less off the tee than a 'warm' one. So hot up your golf on cold days with a warm ball on each hole.

(a) A golf glove which is hard and worn is no help to a golfer. As soon as it begins to feel uncomfortable - change it.

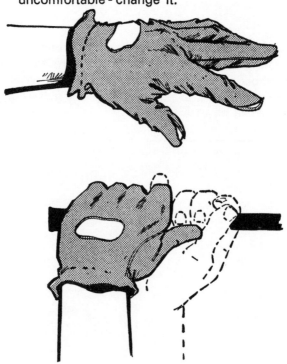

(b) A good glove is the first step to a good grip

23

WINTER EXERCISES

Winter is not the golfer's friend; its heavy snows and dazzling frosts drive him from the course. The wise golfer will take advantage of this forced rest to detect errors in his golf swing and correct them. If it is too cold to attempt this work in the garage, go indoors and get busy in the room least likely to disturb others.

Unfortunately most ceilings are too low for you to execute a full swing. But you can still practise the correct body movements of a full swing without causing any damage. Place a golf ball on the floor and assume your normal stance. Now position the club behind your back, supporting it in the crook of your arms. Keeping your head still turn your body backwards and forwards as you would in a full swing. At the completion of the backswing the clubhead should be pointing down at the ball. Similarly, at the completion of the follow-through it should again be pointing down at the ball. If you find the clubhead is not pointing down you have not rotated your shoulders on the correct plane.

An excellent form of indoor practice is chipping into an armchair. A small piece of cheap matting ensures you do not take divots from your existing carpet. It is best to begin by using plastic balls, things have a nasty habit of going wrong at first, especially when

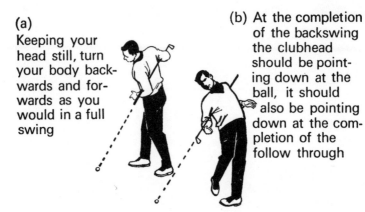

(a) Keeping your head still, turn your body backwards and forwards as you would in a full swing

(b) At the completion of the backswing the clubhead should be pointing down at the ball, it should also be pointing down at the completion of the follow through

the best china is in firing range. When you have mastered these plastic ones change to a real ball. Soon you will find the exercise becoming too easy so reduce your target area. Place a small cardboard box on the armchair and aim to chip the balls inside. Those that miss will be safely caught in the chair, those that drop in the box will stay there if you place an old jumper inside to prevent them from rebounding out.

During tournaments Ben Hogan would spend some time each

A club, laid on the carpet in the direction of the putt, will help you to keep your putting stroke as straight as possible

evening practising putting on the carpet of his hotel room. Putting on the carpet using a chair leg or tumbler as the target is an exercise I strongly recommend. This sort of practice instills the same sense of rhythm and timing needed out there on the greens. Treat these workouts seriously; putting over a carpet provides conditions which closely resemble the real thing, even if the ball does run rather fast, so concentrate and try to hole each putt. A club laid on the carpet in the direction of the putt will help you to keep your putting stroke as straight as possible. A word of warning—a little movement of the head can send your putt a long way off line, so keep it still. During the 1961 British Open, Arnold Palmer was missing out on the greens until his wife, Winnie, told him he was moving his head. Arnie took her advice, started dropping his putts again and won the tournament.

All you need to strengthen your hands, fingers and wrists is a broomstick, a piece of string and a heavy weight. Measure half way down the broomstick and bore a hole. Carefully thread a piece of string through the hole and tie a weight to the end of it. Now with your hands apart, hold the stick parallel to the ground and start winding. Raise the weight up to the stick, then slowly lower it down to the floor again. Repeat this twelve to fifteen times.

A few gentle exercises are needed if you want to keep in reasonable trim during the winter idleness. It is essential to keep the back loose and the simplest method of doing this is to stand erect and then reach down to touch your toes. Don't cheat, keep those knees straight. Strong man Gary Player does seventy fingertip press-ups a day—to make it a little more interesting he will, at times, do this with his wife on his back.

TAKE A TIP . . .

Strong hands, wrists and fingers are essential if you are to retain a correct and constant grip in every phase of the swing. Make a point to do hand strengthening exercises at least once a week.

24

THE RULES

Make sure you are thoroughly familiar with the rules of your local course. When you are playing away at another club, obtain a copy of the local rules, the chances are they will be different from your own. These rules are usually printed on your score card, so study them before you tee off. Ignorance of the rules is no excuse.

Just how important knowing the rules is can be best illustrated by the story of Arnold Palmer when he won his first Masters' Championship in 1958. In the last round, Palmer's iron shot on the par three twelfth hole was embedded in the soggy ground just off the green. The heavy rains which had brought about these conditions had produced a local ruling which clearly stated that a buried ball could be dropped without penalty. To verify this new ruling Palmer checked with an official and was surprised to be told he had to play it as it lied. Palmer, convinced that the official was wrong, said so and then proceeded to take four shots to get the ball down from the thick mud. He then went back to where his ball had been buried, dropped a provisional, chipped up and one-putted for his par three. The decision was upheld in Palmer's favour and he won the tournament. His winning margin . . . . one stroke.

The casual-water rule is one that most club golfers find extremely helpful. Briefly it is this: if your ball lies in casual water on the green or casual water intervenes between it and the hole, the ball may be lifted and placed, without penalty, on the nearest spot (not nearer the hole) which will give you a clear line to the hole. Also if your feet are in casual water you can lift and drop; the lie may be bad and you may feel you are cheating a bit but that's the rule—if you don't use it, your opponent might.

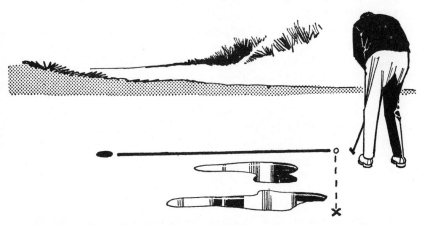

If your ball lies in casual water on the green, or casual water intervenes between it and the hole, the ball may be lifted and placed, without penalty, on the nearest spot (not nearer the hole) which will give you a clear line to the hole

Another point to remember is always to check before a round that you have different-numbered balls in your bag. If you've only got identical-numbered balls you're in trouble. For example, if you drive a ball into the bushes and it looks as if it's lost, you play another. But once again misfortune befalls you and this, too, goes into the bushes, apparently lost. The next one you drive lands safely in the middle of the fairway. Now should you be lucky enough to find the first two balls who is to say which is the one you hit first? The situation becomes trickier when you discover one is in an open space and the other unplayable.

Knowing the rules is one thing, keeping them is another. Golf is the only game where you frequently have to pass rulings on yourself. There will be occasions when only you know if the ball moved as you addressed it, or if your club touched the sand in a bunker. In the 1925 U.S. Open Bobby Jones insisted on penalising himself a stroke when his ball accidentally moved in the rough when the blade of his iron touched the grass. No one else saw the ball move, and the officials wanted to waive the incident. But Jones insisted. That stroke cost him the title and eventually prevented him from becoming the only man ever to win five U.S. Opens. When Jones was praised for this incident, he became indignant: 'There is only one way to play the game,' he said. 'You might as well praise a man for not robbing a bank!'

The Americans are a great more rule conscious than we are. For instance, if your ball goes in the rough, many of them will march over to have a look at it with you. They are there checking everything is done according to the rule book. When this happens to me I find it very annoying and I simply ignore them. Personally I feel there are occasions when some players go too far in this respect— knowing the rules is a must, but becoming a golf course lawyer isn't.

On the putting green you are allowed to repair a pitch mark but not spike marks, yet you will find some golfers go along and knock all the marks down with their putter. Now this is fine if everybody is going to do it, as it is only the rule bender gets the advantage. But to come straight out and accuse someone of cheating is a serious affair and it can have far reaching effects. You must be one hundred per cent certain he is breaking the rules before you say anything. We are professionals, we should know the rules, we *know* if we do something wrong, there shouldn't be any case for some golfers assuming the role of school teacher.

Let me end with a story I was told many years ago. Apparently a golfer—who shall be nameless—had the annoying habit of putting down a six when he had, in fact, taken a seven, a five when he had taken a six, and so on. Then came the day when he actually holed in one. The occasion almost proved too much for him, but not quite, for undeterred down on his card went o.